HOUSING (WALES) ACT 2014 (UK)

Updated as of April 23, 2018

THE LAW LIBRARY

TABLE OF CONTENTS

Introductory Text	4
PART 1. REGULATION OF PRIVATE RENTED HOUSING	4
Interpretation of this Part and index of defined terms	31
PART 2. HOMELESSNESS	32
PART 3. GYPSIES AND TRAVELLERS	59
PART 4. STANDARDS FOR SOCIAL HOUSING	62
PART 5. HOUSING FINANCE	67
PART 6. ALLOWING FULLY MUTUAL HOUSING ASSOCIATIONS TO GRANT ASSURED TENANCIES	70
PART 7. COUNCIL TAX FOR CERTAIN TYPES OF DWELLING	71
PART 8. AMENDMENT OF THE LEASEHOLD REFORM, HOUSING AND URBAN DEVELOPMENT ACT 1993	73
PART 9. MISCELLANEOUS AND GENERAL	73
Schedules	75
Schedule 1. REGISTER OF PRIVATE RENTED HOUSING	75
Schedule 2. ELIGIBILITY FOR HELP UNDER CHAPTER 2 OF PART 2	77
Schedule 3. MINOR AND CONSEQUENTIAL AMENDMENTS	78
Open Government Licence v3.0	85

Introductory Text

Housing (Wales) Act 2014

2014 anaw 7

An Act of the National Assembly for Wales to provide for the regulation of private rented housing; to reform the law relating to homelessness; to provide for assessment of the accommodation needs of Gypsies and Travellers and to require local authorities to meet those needs; to make provision about the standards of housing provided by local authorities; to abolish housing revenue account subsidy; to allow fully mutual housing associations to grant assured tenancies; to make provision about council tax payable for empty dwellings; and for other housing purposes.
[17 September 2014]
Having been passed by the National Assembly for Wales and having received the assent of Her Majesty, it is enacted as follows:

PART 1. REGULATION OF PRIVATE RENTED HOUSING

PART 1 REGULATION OF PRIVATE RENTED HOUSING

1. Overview of this Part

(1) This Part regulates—
　(a) the letting of dwellings under certain kinds of tenancy (which are defined as "domestic tenancies" in section 2), and
　(b) the management of dwellings subject to such tenancies,
by means of a system of registration and licensing.
(2) It requires landlords to be—
　(a) registered for each dwelling subject to, or marketed or offered for let under, a domestic tenancy in respect of which they are the landlord (section 4), subject to exceptions (section 5);
　(b) licensed to carry out certain kinds of lettings activities for dwellings marketed or offered for let under domestic tenancies (section 6), subject to exceptions (section 8);
　(c) licensed to carry out certain kinds of property management activities for dwellings subject to a domestic tenancy (section 7), subject to exceptions (section 8).
(3) It requires persons acting on behalf of a landlord to be licensed to carry out—
　(a) lettings work in respect of a dwelling marketed or offered for let under a domestic tenancy (section 9);
　(b) property management work in respect of a dwelling subject to a domestic tenancy (section 11).

(4) "Lettings work" and "property management work" are defined for the purposes of the Part in sections 10 and 12; the definitions exclude certain persons and activities from the licensing requirements imposed on persons acting on behalf of landlords.

(5) The system of registration and licensing is to be administered and enforced by a person designated by the Welsh Ministers as the licensing authority for the whole of Wales or by different persons designated as licensing authorities for different areas within Wales (section 3); provision is also made for local housing authorities to exercise certain enforcement powers.

(6) Sections 14 to 17 and Schedule 1 provide for a register to be established and maintained by the licensing authority and for registration generally.

(7) Sections 18 to 27 provide for licences generally; and

(a) a licensing authority may only grant two kinds of licence (one for landlords and the other for persons acting on behalf of landlords) and licences have effect in respect of the area for which a licensing authority is responsible (section 18);

(b) in order to be licensed a person must meet certain criteria, including being a fit and proper person (section 20) and requirements relating to training (see section 19).

(8) The requirements imposed by this Part are enforced by—

(a) offences for contravention of registration and licensing requirements (see sections referred to in subsections (2) and (3) and sections 16. (3), 23. (3), 38. (1) and (4) and 39. (1) and (2));

(b) fixed penalty notices (section 29);

(c) rent stopping orders (sections 30 and 31);

(d) rent repayment orders (sections 32 and 33).

(9) Sections 36 to 39 make provision about information required or given for the purposes of this Part.

(10) Section 40 provides for the Welsh Ministers to issue a code of practice and provision is made for guidance (section 41) and directions (section 42).

(11) Sections 43 to 48 make supplementary provision.

(12) Section 49 makes further provision about interpretation and indexes the defined terms used in this Part.

Commencement Information

I1. S. 1 in force at 23.11.2015 by S.I. 2015/1826, art. 2. (a)

2. Meaning of key terms

(1) In this Part—
"domestic tenancy" ("tenantiaeth ddomestig") means—

- a tenancy which is an assured tenancy for the purposes of the Housing Act 1988 (which includes an assured shorthold tenancy), except where the tenancy—

is a long lease for the purposes of Chapter 1 of Part 1 of the Leasehold Reform, Housing and Urban Development Act 1993 ("the 1993 Act"), or

in the case of a shared ownership lease (within the meaning given by section 7. (7) of the 1993 Act), would be such a lease if the tenant's share (within the meaning given by that section) were 100 per cent;

- a regulated tenancy for the purposes of the Rent Act 1977, or

- a tenancy under which a dwelling is let as a separate dwelling and which is of a description specified for the purposes of this Part in an order made by the Welsh Ministers;

"dwelling" ("annedd") means a building or part of a building occupied or intended to be occupied as a separate dwelling, together with any yard, garden, outhouses and appurtenances belonging to it or usually enjoyed with it, where the whole of the dwelling is in Wales;

"landlord" ("landlord") means—

- in relation to a dwelling subject to a domestic tenancy, the immediate landlord or, in relation to a statutory tenant, the person who, apart from the statutory tenancy, would be entitled to possession of the dwelling subject to the tenancy, and

- in relation to a dwelling that is not subject to a domestic tenancy, the person who would be the immediate landlord if the dwelling were let under a domestic tenancy;
"rental property" ("eiddo ar rent") means a dwelling subject to, or marketed or offered for let under, a domestic tenancy.
(2) In this section, "statutory tenant" and "statutory tenancy" mean a statutory tenant or statutory tenancy within the meaning of the Rent Act 1977.
Commencement Information
I2. S. 2 in force at 1.12.2014 for specified purposes by S.I. 2014/3127, art. 2. (b), Sch. Pt. 2
I3. S. 2 in force at 23.11.2015 in so far as not already in force by S.I. 2015/1826, art. 2. (b)

3. Licensing authority

(1) For the purposes of this Part, the Welsh Ministers must by order—
    (a) designate one person as the licensing authority for the whole of Wales, or
    (b) designate different persons as licensing authorities for different areas of Wales specified in the order, provided that each area has no more than one licensing authority and that all of the areas taken together comprise the whole of Wales.
(2) The Welsh Ministers—
    (a) may only designate a person who exercises functions of a public nature wholly or mainly in relation to Wales;
    (b) may designate themselves;
    (c) may not designate a Minister of the Crown.
(3) The Welsh Ministers may by order make any provision they consider necessary or expedient in connection with the designation of a person under this section.
(4) Before making an order under subsection, the Welsh Ministers must consult any person whom they propose to designate (except themselves) and such other persons as the Welsh Ministers consider appropriate.
Commencement Information
I4. S. 3 in force at 1.12.2014 for specified purposes by S.I. 2014/3127, art. 2. (b), Sch. Pt. 2
I5. S. 3 in force at 23.11.2015 in so far as not already in force by S.I. 2015/1826, art. 2. (c)

Prohibition of letting and management without registration and licence

4. Requirement for a landlord to be registered

(1) The landlord of a dwelling subject to, or marketed or offered for let under, a domestic tenancy must be registered under this Part in respect of the dwelling (see sections 14 to 17), unless an exception in section 5 applies.
(2) A landlord who contravenes subsection (1) commits an offence and is liable on summary conviction to a fine not exceeding level 3 on the standard scale.
(3) In proceedings against a landlord for an offence under subsection (2) it is a defence that the landlord has a reasonable excuse for not being registered.
Commencement Information
I6. S. 4 in force at 23.11.2016 by S.I. 2016/1066, art. 2

5. Exceptions to the requirement for a landlord to be registered

The requirement in section 4. (1) does not apply—
    (a) if the landlord has applied to the licensing authority to be registered in relation to that

dwelling and the application has not been determined;
   (b) for a period of 28 days beginning with the date the landlord's interest in the dwelling is assigned to the landlord;
   (c) if the landlord takes steps to recover possession of the dwelling within a period of 28 days beginning with the date the landlord's interest in the dwelling is assigned to the landlord, for so long as the landlord continues to diligently pursue the recovery of possession;
   (d) to a landlord who is a registered social landlord;
   (e) to a landlord who is a fully mutual housing association;
   (f) to a person of a description specified for the purposes of this section in an order made by the Welsh Ministers.

Commencement Information
I7. S. 5 in force at 1.12.2014 for specified purposes by S.I. 2014/3127, art. 2. (b), Sch. Pt. 2
I8. S. 5 in force at 23.11.2016 in so far as not already in force by S.I. 2016/1066, art. 2

6. Requirement for landlords to be licensed to carry out lettings activities

(1) The landlord of a dwelling marketed or offered for let under a domestic tenancy must not do any of the things described in subsection (2) in respect of the dwelling unless—
   (a) the landlord is licensed to do so under this Part for the area in which the dwelling is located,
   (b) the thing done is arranging for an authorised agent to do something on the landlord's behalf, or
   (c) an exception in section 8 applies.

(2) The things are—
   (a) arranging or conducting viewings with prospective tenants;
   (b) gathering evidence for the purpose of establishing the suitability of prospective tenants (for example, by confirming character references, undertaking credit checks or interviewing a prospective tenant);
   (c) preparing, or arranging the preparation, of a tenancy agreement;
   (d) preparing, or arranging the preparation, of an inventory for the dwelling or schedule of condition for the dwelling.

(3) The Welsh Ministers may by order—
   (a) amend or omit the descriptions of things in subsection (2) (including things added under paragraph (b));
   (b) add further descriptions of things to subsection (2).

(4) A landlord who contravenes subsection (1) commits an offence and is liable on summary conviction to a fine.

(5) In proceedings against a landlord for an offence under subsection (4) it is a defence that the landlord has a reasonable excuse for not being licensed.

(6) In subsection (1) "authorised agent" means—
   (a) a person licensed to carry out lettings work and property management work under this Part for the area in which the dwelling is located,
   (b) a local housing authority (whether or not in exercise of its functions as a local housing authority), or
   (c) in relation to preparing, or arranging the preparation of a tenancy agreement only, a qualified solicitor (within the meaning of Part 1 of the Solicitors Act 1974), a person acting on behalf of such a solicitor or any person of a description specified in an order made by the Welsh Ministers.

Commencement Information
I9. S. 6 in force at 1.12.2014 for specified purposes by S.I. 2014/3127, art. 2. (b), Sch. Pt. 2
I10. S. 6 in force at 23.11.2016 in so far as not already in force by S.I. 2016/1066, art. 2

7. Requirement for landlords to be licensed to carry out property management activities

(1) The landlord of a dwelling subject to a domestic tenancy must not do any of the things described in subsection (2) in respect of the dwelling unless—
   (a) the landlord is licensed to do so under this Part for the area in which the dwelling is located,
   (b) the thing done is arranging for an authorised agent to do something on the landlord's behalf, or
   (c) an exception in section 8 applies.
(2) The things are—
   (a) collecting rent;
   (b) being the principal point of contact for the tenant in relation to matters arising under the tenancy;
   (c) making arrangements with a person to carry out repairs or maintenance;
   (d) making arrangements with a tenant or occupier of the dwelling to secure access to the dwelling for any purpose;
   (e) checking the contents or condition of the dwelling, or arranging for them to be checked;
   (f) serving notice to terminate a tenancy.
(3) The landlord of a dwelling that was subject to a domestic tenancy, but is no longer subject to that domestic tenancy, must not check the contents or condition of the dwelling, or arrange for them to be checked, for any purpose connected with that tenancy unless—
   (a) the landlord is licensed to do so under this Part for the area in which the dwelling is located,
   (b) the thing done is arranging for an authorised agent to do it on the landlord's behalf, or
   (c) an exception in section 8 applies.
(4) The Welsh Ministers may by order—
   (a) amend or omit the descriptions of things in subsection (2) or (3) (including things added under paragraph (b)) that a landlord must not do unless any of paragraphs (a) to (c) of subsection (1) or (3) applies (as the case may be);
   (b) add further descriptions of things for the purposes of this section (including by way of amendment to this Part).
(5) A landlord who contravenes subsection (1) or (3) commits an offence and is liable on summary conviction to a fine.
(6) In proceedings against a landlord for an offence under subsection (5) it is a defence that the landlord has a reasonable excuse for not being licensed.
(7) In subsection (1) "authorised agent" means—
   (a) a person licensed to carry out lettings work and property management work under this Part for the area in which the dwelling is located,
   (b) a local housing authority (whether or not in exercise of its functions as a local housing authority), or
   (c) in relation to serving notice to terminate a tenancy only, a qualified solicitor (within the meaning of Part 1 of the Solicitors Act 1974), a person acting on behalf of such a solicitor or any person of a description specified in an order made by the Welsh Ministers.
Commencement Information
I11. S. 7 in force at 1.12.2014 for specified purposes by S.I. 2014/3127, art. 2. (b), Sch. Pt. 2
I12. S. 7 in force at 23.11.2016 in so far as not already in force by S.I. 2016/1066, art. 2

8. Exceptions to requirements for landlords to be licensed

The requirements in sections 6. (1), 7. (1) and 7. (3) do not apply—
   (a) if the landlord has applied to the licensing authority to be licensed, for the period from the date of the application until it is determined by the authority or (if the authority refuses the

application) until all means of appealing against a decision to refuse an application have been exhausted and the decision is upheld;
 (b) for a period of 28 days beginning with the date the landlord's interest in the dwelling is assigned to the landlord;
 (c) if the landlord takes steps to recover possession of the dwelling within a period of 28 days beginning with the date the landlord's interest in the dwelling is assigned to the landlord, for so long as the landlord continues to diligently pursue the recovery of possession;
 (d) to a landlord who is a registered social landlord;
 (e) to a landlord who is a fully mutual housing association;
 (f) in cases specified for the purposes of this section in an order made by the Welsh Ministers.
Commencement Information
I13. S. 8 in force at 1.12.2014 for specified purposes by S.I. 2014/3127, art. 2. (b), Sch. Pt. 2
I14. S. 8 in force at 23.11.2016 in so far as not already in force by S.I. 2016/1066, art. 2

9. Requirement for agents to be licensed to carry out lettings work

(1) A person acting on behalf of the landlord of a dwelling marketed or offered for let under a domestic tenancy must not carry out lettings work in respect of the dwelling unless the person is licensed to do so under this Part for the area in which the dwelling is located.
(2) A person who contravenes this section commits an offence and is liable on summary conviction to a fine.
(3) In proceedings against a person for an offence committed under subsection (2) it is a defence that the person has a reasonable excuse for not being licensed.
Commencement Information
I15. S. 9 in force at 23.11.2016 by S.I. 2016/1066, art. 2

10. Meaning of lettings work

(1) In this Part "lettings work" means things done by any person in response to instructions received from—
 (a) a person seeking to find another person wishing to rent a dwelling under a domestic tenancy and, having found such a person, to grant such a tenancy ("a prospective landlord");
 (b) a person seeking to find a dwelling to rent under a domestic tenancy and, having found such a dwelling, to obtain such a tenancy of it ("a prospective tenant");
subject to the following subsections.
(2) "Lettings work" does not include anything in the following paragraphs (a) or (b)—
 (a) publishing advertisements or disseminating information;
 (b) providing a means by which—
(i) a prospective landlord (or the prospective landlord's agent) or a prospective tenant can, in response to an advertisement or dissemination of information, make direct contact with a prospective tenant or (as the case may be) prospective landlord (or the prospective landlord's agent);
(ii) a prospective landlord (or the prospective landlord's agent) and a prospective tenant can continue to communicate directly with each other;
when done by a person who—
 (c) does no other thing within subsection (1), and
 (d) does no property management work in respect of the property.
(3) "Lettings work" does not include doing any one of the things in the following paragraphs (a) to (c)—
 (a) arranging and conducting viewings with prospective tenants;
 (b) preparing, or arranging the preparation of, the tenancy agreement;
 (c) preparing, or arranging the preparation of, any inventory or schedule of condition;

when done by a person who—
(d) does no other thing in those paragraphs or anything else within subsection (1), and
(e) does nothing within section 12. (1) in respect of the property.
(4) "Lettings work" also does not include—
(a) doing things under a contract of service or apprenticeship with a landlord;
(b) doing things under a contract of service or apprenticeship, or a contract for services, with a person who is—
(i) instructed to carry out the work by a landlord, and
(ii) licensed to do so under this Part;
(c) anything done by a local housing authority (whether or not in exercise of its functions as a local housing authority);
(d) things of a description, or things done by a person of a description, specified for the purposes of this section in an order made by the Welsh Ministers.

Commencement Information
I16. S. 10 in force at 1.12.2014 for specified purposes by S.I. 2014/3127, art. 2. (b), Sch. Pt. 2
I17. S. 10 in force at 23.11.2016 in so far as not already in force by S.I. 2016/1066, art. 2

11. Requirement for agents to be licensed to carry out property management work

(1) A person acting on behalf of the landlord of a dwelling subject to a domestic tenancy must not carry out property management work in respect of the dwelling unless the person is licensed to do so under this Part for the area in which the dwelling is located.
(2) Where a dwelling was subject to a domestic tenancy, but is no longer subject to that domestic tenancy, a person acting on behalf of the landlord of the dwelling must not check the contents or condition of the dwelling, or arrange for them to be checked, for any purpose connected with that tenancy unless—
(a) the person is licensed to do so under this Part for the area in which the dwelling is located,
(b) the person does no other thing in respect of the dwelling falling within—
(i) section 10. (1), except preparing, or arranging the preparation of, any inventory or schedule of condition, or
(ii) section 12. (1), or
(c) the activity would not, by virtue of section 12. (3), be property management work.
(3) A person who contravenes subsection (1) or (2) commits an offence and is liable on summary conviction to a fine.
(4) In proceedings against a person for an offence committed under subsection (3) it is a defence that the person has a reasonable excuse for not being licensed.

Commencement Information
I18. S. 11 in force at 23.11.2016 by S.I. 2016/1066, art. 2

12. Meaning of property management work

(1) In this Part, "property management work" means doing any of the following things—
(a) collecting rent;
(b) being the principal point of contact for the tenant in relation to matters arising under the tenancy;
(c) making arrangements with a person to carry out repairs or maintenance;
(d) making arrangements with a tenant or occupier of the dwelling to secure access to the dwelling for any purpose;
(e) checking the contents or condition of the dwelling, or arranging for them to be checked;
(f) serving notice to terminate a tenancy.

(2) But "property management work" does not include doing any one of the things in paragraphs (b) to (f) of subsection (1) when done by a person who—
  (a) does no other thing within subsection (1), and
  (b) does nothing within section 10. (1) in respect of the dwelling.
(3) "Property management work" also does not include—
  (a) doing things under a contract of service or apprenticeship with a landlord;
  (b) doing things under a contract of service or apprenticeship, or a contract for services, with a person who is—
(i) instructed to carry out the work by a landlord, and
(ii) licensed to do so under this Part;
  (c) anything done by a local housing authority (whether or not in exercise of its functions as a local housing authority);
  (d) things of a description, or things done by a person of a description, specified for the purposes of this section in an order made by the Welsh Ministers.
Commencement Information
I19. S. 12 in force at 1.12.2014 for specified purposes by S.I. 2014/3127, art. 2. (b), Sch. Pt. 2
I20. S. 12 in force at 23.11.2016 in so far as not already in force by S.I. 2016/1066, art. 2

13. Offence of appointing an unlicensed agent

(1) The landlord of a dwelling marketed or offered for let under a domestic tenancy must not appoint or continue to allow a person to undertake lettings work on behalf of the landlord in relation to that dwelling, if—
  (a) the person does not hold a licence to do so under this Part for the area in which the dwelling is located, and
  (b) the landlord knows or should know that the person does not hold such a licence.
(2) The landlord of a dwelling subject to a domestic tenancy must not appoint or continue to allow a person to undertake property management work on behalf of the landlord in relation to that dwelling, if—
  (a) the person does not hold a licence to do so under this Part for the area in which the dwelling is located, and
  (b) the landlord knows or should know that the person does not hold such a licence.
(3) A landlord who contravenes subsection (1) or (2) commits an offence and is liable on summary conviction to a fine not exceeding level 4 on the standard scale.
Commencement Information
I21. S. 13 in force at 23.11.2016 by S.I. 2016/1066, art. 2

Registration

14. Duty to maintain register in relation to rental properties

(1) A licensing authority must establish and maintain a register for its area containing the information set out in Part 1 of Schedule 1.
(2) Part 2 of Schedule 1 contains provision relating to public access to information held on the register.
(3) The Welsh Ministers may amend Schedule 1 by order.
Commencement Information
I22. S. 14 in force at 1.12.2014 for specified purposes by S.I. 2014/3127, art. 2. (b), Sch. Pt. 2
I23. S. 14 in force at 23.11.2015 in so far as not already in force by S.I. 2015/1826, art. 2. (d)

15. Registration by a licensing authority

(1) An application for registration is to be made to the licensing authority for the area in which the dwelling to which the application relates is located; and the authority must register the landlord within the prescribed period if the application—
    (a) is made in the form required by the authority,
    (b) includes such information as is prescribed,
    (c) includes such other information as the authority requires, and
    (d) is accompanied by the prescribed fee.
(2) If the landlord is registered, the licensing authority must notify the landlord—
    (a) that the landlord is registered, and
    (b) of the registration number assigned to the landlord.
(3) On the first occasion a landlord is registered a licensing authority must assign a registration number to the landlord.
(4) A licensing authority may charge the landlord a further prescribed fee for continued registration—
    (a) after the fifth anniversary of the date the landlord was registered, and
    (b) after every fifth anniversary of the date a further prescribed fee was charged.
Commencement Information
I24. S. 15 in force at 1.12.2014 for specified purposes by S.I. 2014/3127, art. 2. (b), Sch. Pt. 2
I25. S. 15 in force at 23.11.2015 in so far as not already in force by S.I. 2015/1826, art. 2. (e)

16. Duty to update information

(1) A landlord who is registered under section 15 in relation to a rental property must notify the licensing authority in writing of the following changes—
    (a) any change in the name under which the landlord is registered;
    (b) the appointment of a person to carry out lettings work or property management work on behalf of the landlord in respect of the rental property;
    (c) that a person who the landlord has previously appointed to carry out lettings work or property management work on behalf of the landlord in respect of the rental property has ceased to do so;
    (d) any assignment of the landlord's interest in the rental property;
    (e) any prescribed changes.
(2) A landlord must comply with the duty in subsection (1) within 28 days beginning with the first day on which the landlord knew, or should have known, of the change.
(3) A person who contravenes subsection (1) commits an offence and is liable on summary conviction to a fine not exceeding level 1 on the standard scale.
(4) In proceedings against a person for an offence committed under subsection (3) it is a defence that the person had a reasonable excuse for failing to comply.
Commencement Information
I26. S. 16 in force at 1.12.2014 for specified purposes by S.I. 2014/3127, art. 2. (b), Sch. Pt. 2
I27. S. 16 in force at 23.11.2015 in so far as not already in force by S.I. 2015/1826, art. 2. (f)

17. Revocation of registration

(1) A licensing authority may revoke the registration of any landlord who—
    (a) provides false or misleading information in an application under section 15 or in notifying a change under section 16;
    (b) contravenes section 16;
    (c) fails to pay any further fee charged under section 15.

(2) Before revoking a landlord's registration a licensing authority must—
    (a) notify the landlord of its intention to revoke the registration and the reasons for this, and
    (b) consider any representations made by the landlord before the end of the period of 21 days beginning with the date the landlord was notified.
(3) After revoking a landlord's registration a licensing authority must notify the landlord—
    (a) of the revocation and the reasons for doing so;
    (b) of the landlord's right of appeal.
(4) A person whose registration is revoked may appeal against the decision to a residential property tribunal.
(5) An appeal—
    (a) must be made before the end of the period of 28 days beginning with the date on which the person was notified of the decision (the "appeal period");
    (b) may be determined having regard to matters of which the licensing authority was unaware.
(6) The tribunal may allow an appeal to be made to it after the end of the appeal period if it is satisfied that there is a good reason for the failure to appeal before the end of that period (and for any delay in applying for permission to appeal out of time).
(7) The tribunal may confirm the decision of the licensing authority or direct the authority to register the landlord.
(8) Revocation of a landlord's registration takes effect on the day whichever of the following first occurs—
    (a) where the landlord does not appeal against the decision to revoke the registration within the appeal period, the expiry of that period;
    (b) where the landlord appeals within the appeal period but later withdraws the appeal, the date of the withdrawal;
    (c) where the landlord appeals within the appeal period and the residential property tribunal confirms the decision of the licensing authority, subject to paragraph (d), the date of the tribunal's decision;
    (d) where the landlord makes a further appeal, the date on which all means of appealing against the decision have been exhausted and the licensing authority's decision is upheld.
(9) Where a landlord's registration is revoked, the licensing authority must—
    (a) notify any person recorded on the register as having been appointed by the landlord to carry out lettings work or property management work on behalf of the landlord, and
    (b) notify the tenants or occupiers of rental properties registered under the landlord's name.
Commencement Information
I28. S. 17 in force at 23.11.2015 by S.I. 2015/1826, art. 2. (g)

Licensing

18. Licences that may be granted

A licensing authority may only grant the following kinds of licence under this Part—
    (a) a licence for its area for the purpose of compliance with sections 6 (requirement for landlords to be licensed to carry out lettings activities) and 7 (requirement for landlords to be licensed to carry out property management activities);
    (b) a licence for its area for the purpose of compliance with sections 9 (requirement for agents to be licensed to carry out lettings work) and 11 (requirement for agents to be licensed to carry out property management work).
Commencement Information
I29. S. 18 in force at 23.11.2015 by S.I. 2015/1826, art. 2. (h)

19. Licence application requirements

(1) An application for a licence must—
   (a) be made in such form as is required by the licensing authority,
   (b) provide such information as is prescribed,
   (c) provide such other information as the authority requires, and
   (d) be accompanied by the prescribed fee.
(2) Before granting a licence a licensing authority must be satisfied—
   (a) that the applicant is a fit and proper person to be licensed (see section 20);
   (b) that requirements in relation to training specified in or under regulations made by the Welsh Ministers are met or will be met (as the case may be).
(3) Regulations made under subsection (2)(b) may (among other things)—
   (a) authorise a licensing authority to specify requirements in relation to training in respect of—
(i) the statutory obligations of a landlord and a tenant;
(ii) the contractual relationship between a landlord and a tenant;
(iii) the role of an agent who carries out lettings work or property management work;
(iv) best practice in letting and managing dwellings subject to, or marketed or offered for let under, a domestic tenancy;
   (b) make provision for and in connection with requiring training—
(i) to be carried out by persons authorised to do so by the licensing authority or the Welsh Ministers;
(ii) to be delivered through training courses approved by the licensing authority or the Welsh Ministers;
this includes the power to make provision for charging fees for authorisation or approval.
Commencement Information
I30. S. 19 in force at 1.12.2014 for specified purposes by S.I. 2014/3127, art. 2. (b), Sch. Pt. 2
I31. S. 19 in force at 23.11.2015 in so far as not already in force by S.I. 2015/1826, art. 2. (i)

20. Fit and proper person requirement

(1) In deciding whether a person is a fit and proper person to be licensed as required by section 19. (2)(a), a licensing authority must have regard to all matters it considers appropriate.
(2) Among the matters to which the licensing authority must have regard is any evidence within subsections (3) to (5).
(3) Evidence is within this subsection if it shows that the person has—
   (a) committed any offence involving fraud or other dishonesty, violence, firearms or drugs or any offence listed in Schedule 3 to the Sexual Offences Act 2003 (offences attracting notification requirements),
   (b) practised unlawful discrimination or harassment on the grounds of any characteristic which is a protected characteristic under section 4 of the Equality Act 2010, or victimised another person contrary to that Act, in or in connection with the carrying on of any business, or
   (c) contravened any provision of the law relating to housing or landlord and tenant.
(4) Evidence is within this subsection if—
   (a) it shows that any other person associated or formerly associated with the person (whether on a personal, work or other basis) has done any of the things set out in subsection (3), and
   (b) it appears to the licensing authority that the evidence is relevant to the question whether the person is a fit and proper person to be licensed.
(5) Evidence is within this subsection if it shows the person has previously failed to comply with a condition of a licence granted under this Part by a licensing authority.
(6) The Welsh Ministers must give guidance to licensing authorities about deciding whether a person is a fit and proper person to be licensed as required by section 19. (2)(a).
(7) The Welsh Ministers may amend this section by order to vary the evidence to which a

licensing authority must have regard in deciding whether a person is a fit and proper person to be licensed.
Commencement Information
I32. S. 20 in force at 1.12.2014 for specified purposes by S.I. 2014/3127, art. 2. (b), Sch. Pt. 2
I33. S. 20 in force at 1.12.2014 for specified purposes by S.I. 2014/3127, art. 2. (c), Sch. Pt. 3
I34. S. 20 in force at 23.11.2015 in so far as not already in force by S.I. 2015/1826, art. 2. (j)

21. Determination of application

(1) Where a licensing authority is satisfied that the applicant meets the requirements set out in section 19, it must grant a licence to the applicant.
(2) After granting the licence the licensing authority must—
    (a) assign a licence number to the licence holder;
    (b) record the licence number in the licence;
    (c) record the date the licence was granted in the licence;
    (d) give the licence to the licence holder.
(3) Where a licensing authority refuses an application, it must notify the applicant—
    (a) that the application has been refused and the reasons why;
    (b) of the applicant's right to appeal (see section 27).
(4) An application must be determined by the licensing authority within a prescribed period.
Commencement Information
I35. S. 21 in force at 1.12.2014 for specified purposes by S.I. 2014/3127, art. 2. (b), Sch. Pt. 2
I36. S. 21 in force at 23.11.2015 in so far as not already in force by S.I. 2015/1826, art. 2. (k)

22. Licence conditions

(1) A licence must be granted subject to a condition that the licence holder complies with any code of practice issued by the Welsh Ministers under section 40.
(2) A licensing authority may grant a licence subject to such further conditions as it considers appropriate.
Commencement Information
I37. S. 22 in force at 23.11.2015 by S.I. 2015/1826, art. 2. (l)

23. Duty to update information

(1) A licence holder must notify the licensing authority in writing of the following changes—
    (a) any change in the name under which the licence holder is licensed;
    (b) any prescribed changes.
(2) A licence holder must comply with the duty in subsection (1) within 28 days beginning with the first day on which the licence holder knew, or should have known, of the change.
(3) A person who contravenes this section commits an offence and is liable on summary conviction to a fine not exceeding level 4 on the standard scale.
(4) In proceedings against a person for an offence committed under subsection (3) it is a defence that the person had a reasonable excuse for failing to comply.
Commencement Information
I38. S. 23 in force at 1.12.2014 for specified purposes by S.I. 2014/3127, art. 2. (b), Sch. Pt. 2
I39. S. 23 in force at 23.11.2015 in so far as not already in force by S.I. 2015/1826, art. 2. (m)

24. Amendment of licence

(1) A licensing authority may, in accordance with this section, amend any licence granted by it.

(2) A licence may be amended to—
  (a) impose new conditions;
  (b) remove or change existing conditions (other than the requirement to comply with any code of practice issued by the Welsh Ministers).
(3) But before deciding to amend a licence a licensing authority must—
  (a) notify the licence holder of its intention to amend the licence and the reasons for this, and
  (b) consider any representations made by the licence holder before the end of the period of 21 days beginning with the date the licence holder was notified.
(4) Subsection (3)(b) does not apply to an amendment if—
  (a) the licence holder consents to it, or
  (b) the licensing authority considers that there are exceptional circumstances which mean that it needs to be made without delay.
(5) After amending a licence the licensing authority must notify the licence holder of—
  (a) the amendment and the reasons for it;
  (b) except where the licence holder has consented to the amendment, information about the licence holder's right of appeal (see section 27).
(6) An amendment to a licence takes effect on the day whichever of the following first occurs—
  (a) where the licence holder has consented, when the licensing authority notifies the licence holder under subsection (5);
  (b) where the licence holder does not appeal against the decision to amend the licence within the appeal period, the expiry of that period;
  (c) where the licence holder appeals within the appeal period but later withdraws the appeal, the date of the withdrawal;
  (d) where the licence holder appeals within the appeal period and the residential property tribunal confirms the decision of the licensing authority to amend the licence, subject to paragraph (e), the date of the tribunal's decision;
  (e) where the licence holder makes a further appeal, the date on which all means of appealing against the decision have been exhausted and the licensing authority's decision is upheld.
(7) The "appeal period" for the purposes of subsection (6) is the period mentioned in section 27.(3)(a) (licensing appeals).
Commencement Information
I40. S. 24 in force at 23.11.2015 by S.I. 2015/1826, art. 2. (n)

25. Revocation of licence

(1) A licensing authority may revoke a licence if—
  (a) the licence holder has breached a condition of the licence;
  (b) the authority is no longer satisfied that the licence holder is a fit and proper person to hold a licence;
  (c) the licence holder has contravened section 23 (licence holder's duty to update information);
  (d) the licence holder and the licensing authority have agreed that the licence should be revoked.
(2) But before revoking a licence a licensing authority must—
  (a) notify the licence holder of its intention to revoke the licence and the reasons for this, and
  (b) consider any representations made by the licence holder before the end of the period of 21 days beginning with the date the licence holder was notified.
(3) Subsection (2)(b) does not apply—
  (a) if the licence holder consents to the revocation, or
  (b) where the licensing authority considers that there are exceptional circumstances which mean that it needs to be revoked without delay.
(4) After revoking a licence the licensing authority must notify the licence holder—
  (a) of the revocation and the reasons for it;
  (b) of the licence holder's right of appeal (see section 27).

(5) Revocation of a licence takes effect on the day whichever of the following first occurs—
    (a) the licence holder contacts the licensing authority consenting to the revocation;
    (b) where the licence holder does not appeal against the decision to revoke the licence within the appeal period, the expiry of that period;
    (c) where the licence holder appeals within the appeal period but later withdraws the appeal, the date of the withdrawal;
    (d) where the licence holder appeals within the appeal period and the residential property tribunal confirms the decision of the licensing authority to revoke the licence, subject to paragraph (e), the date of the tribunal's decision;
    (e) where the licence holder makes a further appeal, the date on which all means of appealing against the decision have been exhausted and the licensing authority's decision is upheld.
(6) The "appeal period" for the purposes of subsection (5) is the period mentioned in section 27.(3)(a) (licensing appeals).
(7) Where a person's licence to carry out lettings work and property management work on behalf of a landlord is revoked, the licensing authority must notify any landlord recorded on its register as having appointed that person.
(8) Where a landlord's licence is revoked, the licensing authority must notify the tenants or occupiers of rental property registered under the landlord's name.
Commencement Information
I41. S. 25 in force at 23.11.2015 by S.I. 2015/1826, art. 2. (o)

26. Expiry and renewal of licence

(1) A licence expires at the end of a period of 5 years beginning with the date it was granted, unless the licence holder makes an application to renew the licence in accordance with subsection (2).
(2) A licence holder may apply to renew the licence during the period of 84 days before the date the licence would otherwise expire.
(3) Where an application is made to renew a licence in accordance with subsection (2) the licence does not expire until the application is decided and expires only if the application is refused.
(4) An application for renewal of a licence is to be made and determined in accordance with sections 19 (licence application requirements) to 21 (determination of application).
(5) But where a licensing authority renews a licence, the requirement in subsection (2)(a) of section 21 to assign a licence number to the licence holder does not apply.
(6) If an application to renew a licence is refused, the existing licence expires on whichever of the following dates first occurs—
    (a) where the licence holder does not appeal against the refusal within the appeal period, the date of expiry of that period;
    (b) where the licence holder appeals within the appeal period but later withdraws the appeal, the date of the withdrawal;
    (c) where the licence holder appeals within the appeal period and the residential property tribunal confirms the decision of the licensing authority, the date of the tribunal's decision (subject to paragraph (d));
    (d) where the licence holder makes a further appeal, the date on which all means of appealing against the decision have been exhausted and the licensing authority's decision is upheld.
(7) The "appeal period" for the purposes of subsection (6) is the period mentioned in section 27.(3)(a) (licensing appeals).
(8) A licence expires and any renewal application made by the licence holder is treated as having been withdrawn where a licence holder—
    (a) dies;
    (b) in the case of a body corporate, is dissolved.
Commencement Information

I42. S. 26 in force at 23.11.2015 by S.I. 2015/1826, art. 2. (p)

27. Licensing appeals

(1) An applicant for a licence or, as the case may be, the holder of a licence may appeal against the decisions of a licensing authority listed in subsection (2) to a residential property tribunal.
(2) The decisions are—
    (a) granting a licence subject to a condition, other than the requirement to comply with any code of practice issued by the Welsh Ministers;
    (b) refusing an application for a licence;
    (c) amending a licence;
    (d) revoking a licence.
(3) An appeal—
    (a) must be made before the end of the period of 28 days beginning with the date the applicant was notified of the decision (the "appeal period");
    (b) may be determined having regard to matters of which the licensing authority was unaware.
(4) The tribunal may allow an appeal to be made to it after the end of the appeal period if it is satisfied that there is a good reason for the failure to appeal before the end of that period (and for any delay in applying for permission to appeal out of time).
(5) The tribunal may confirm the decision of the licensing authority or alternatively—
    (a) in the case of a decision to grant a licence subject to a condition, direct the authority to grant a licence on such terms as the tribunal considers appropriate;
    (b) in the case of a decision to refuse an application for a licence, direct the authority to grant a licence on such terms as the tribunal considers appropriate;
    (c) in the case of a decision to amend a licence, direct the authority not to amend the licence or to amend the licence on such terms as the tribunal considers appropriate;
    (d) in the case of a decision to revoke a licence, to quash that decision.
(6) A licence granted by a licensing authority following a direction of a tribunal under this section is to be treated as having been granted by the authority under section 21. (1).
Commencement Information
I43. S. 27 in force at 23.11.2015 by S.I. 2015/1826, art. 2. (q)

Enforcement

28. Prosecution by a licensing authority or a local housing authority

(1) A licensing authority may bring criminal proceedings in respect of an offence under —
    (a) section 4. (2), 6. (4), 7. (5), 9. (2), 11. (3) or 13. (3) if the alleged offence arises in respect of a dwelling in the area for which it is the licensing authority;
    (b) section 16. (3) or 23. (3), in respect of information to be provided to the licensing authority;
    (c) subsection (1) or (4) of section 38, in respect of anything required by a notice given by a person authorised by the authority;
    (d) subsection (1) or (2) of section 39, in respect of information supplied to the authority.
(2) A local housing authority that is not the licensing authority for its area may, with the consent of the licensing authority for the area, bring criminal proceedings in respect of an offence under section 4. (2), 6. (4), 7. (5), 9. (2), 11. (3) or 13. (3), if the alleged offence arises in respect of a dwelling in its area.
(3) A licensing authority may give its consent under subsection (2) generally or in specific cases.
(4) This section does not affect—

(a) any other power of the person designated under section 3 to bring legal proceedings;
(b) section 222 of the Local Government Act 1972 (power of local authorities to prosecute or defend legal proceedings).
Commencement Information
I44. S. 28 in force at 23.11.2016 by S.I. 2016/1066, art. 2

29. Fixed penalty notices

(1) Where on any occasion a person authorised in writing for the purpose of this section by a licensing authority has reason to believe that a person has committed an offence under this Part (other than an offence under section 13. (3) or section 38. (4)), the authorised person may, by notice, offer the person the opportunity of discharging any liability to conviction for that offence by payment of a fixed penalty to the authority.
(2) Where a person is given a notice under this section in respect of an offence—
(a) no proceedings may be issued for that offence before the expiration of the period of 21 days following the date of the notice;
(b) the person may not be convicted of the offence if the person pays the fixed penalty before the end of that period.
(3) A notice under this section must—
(a) give such particulars of the circumstances alleged to constitute the offence as are necessary for giving reasonable information of the offence,
(b) state the period during which proceedings will not be taken for the offence,
(c) state the amount of the fixed penalty, and
(d) state the person to whom and the address at which the fixed penalty may be paid.
(4) The fixed penalty payable to a licensing authority under this section is £150 unless the offence is an offence attracting an unlimited fine; in which case, the fixed penalty payable is £250.
(5) The Welsh Ministers may amend subsection (4) by order.
(6) Payment of a fixed penalty may be made by pre-paying and posting a letter containing the amount of the penalty (in cash or otherwise) to the person mentioned in subsection (3)(d) at the address so mentioned; but this does not prevent payment by another method.
(7) Where a letter is posted in accordance with subsection (6) payment is to be regarded as having been made at the time at which the letter would be delivered in the ordinary course of post.
(8) In any proceedings a certificate—
(a) which purports to be signed on behalf of a person authorised for this purpose by the licensing authority, and
(b) states that payment of a fixed penalty was or was not received by a date specified in the certificate,
is evidence of the facts stated.
(9) A licensing authority may use its fixed penalty receipts only for the purposes of its functions relating to the enforcement of this Part.
(10) In this section, "licensing authority" means—
(a) in the case of an offence under section 4. (2), 6. (4), 7. (5), 9. (2) or 11. (3), the licensing authority for the area in which the dwelling to which the offence relates is located;
(b) in the case of an offence under section 16. (3) or 23. (3), the licensing authority to which the information to which the offence relates was provided;
(c) in the case of an offence under section 38. (1), the licensing authority which authorised the person who gave the relevant notice;
(d) in the case of an offence under section 39. (1) or (2), the licensing authority to which the information was supplied.
(11) A local housing authority that is not the licensing authority for its area may, with the consent of the licensing authority for the area, exercise the functions of the licensing authority under this section concurrently with the licensing authority; but only in respect of the offences mentioned in

subsection (10)(a).

(12) And where a local housing authority exercises functions under this section by virtue of subsection (11), the references in subsections (1), (4), (8), (9) and (10)(a) to "licensing authority" are to be read as if they were references to the local housing authority.

Commencement Information

I45. S. 29 in force at 1.12.2014 for specified purposes by S.I. 2014/3127, art. 2. (b), Sch. Pt. 2

I46. S. 29 in force at 23.11.2016 in so far as not already in force by S.I. 2016/1066, art. 2

30. Rent stopping orders

(1) A residential property tribunal may, in accordance with this section, make an order (a "rent stopping order") in relation to a dwelling subject to a domestic tenancy on an application made to it by—
   (a) the licensing authority for the area in which the dwelling is located, or
   (b) the local housing authority for the area in which the dwelling is located.

(2) But a local housing authority may not make an application under subsection (1) without the consent of the licensing authority mentioned in paragraph (a) of that subsection (unless it is the licensing authority); and consent for that purpose may be given generally or in respect of a particular application.

(3) Where the tribunal makes a rent stopping order—
   (a) periodical payments payable in connection with a domestic tenancy of the dwelling which relate to a period, or part of a period, falling between a date specified in the order (the "stopping date") and a date specified by the tribunal when the order is revoked (see section 31. (4)) are stopped,
   (b) an obligation under a domestic tenancy to pay an amount stopped by the order is treated as being met,
   (c) all other rights and obligations under such a tenancy continue unaffected,
   (d) any periodical payments stopped by the order but made by a tenant of the dwelling (whether before or after the stopping date) must be repaid by the landlord, and
   (e) the authority which made the application for the order must give a copy of it to—
(i) the landlord of the dwelling to which the order relates;
(ii) the tenant of the dwelling.

(4) The tribunal may make a rent stopping order only if it is satisfied of the matters mentioned in subsections (5) and (6).

(5) The tribunal must be satisfied that an offence is being committed under section 7. (5) or 13. (3) in relation to the dwelling (whether or not a person has been convicted or charged for the offence).

(6) The tribunal must be satisfied that—
   (a) the authority making the application for the order has given the landlord and the tenant of the dwelling a notice (a "notice of intended proceedings")—
(i) explaining that the authority is proposing to apply for a rent stopping order,
(ii) setting out the reasons why it proposes to do so,
(iii) explaining the effect of a rent stopping order,
(iv) explaining how a rent stopping order may be revoked, and
(v) in the case of a notice given to a landlord, inviting the landlord to make representations to the authority within a period of not less than 28 days specified in the notice,
   (b) the period for making representations has expired, and
   (c) the authority considered any representations made to it within that period by the landlord.

(7) The tribunal may not specify a stopping date for the purpose of subsection (3)(a) which precedes the date on which the rent stopping order is made.

(8) An amount payable by virtue of subsection (3)(d) which is not repaid is recoverable by the tenant as a debt due to the tenant from the landlord.

(9) In subsection (5), the reference to an offence committed under section 13. (3) does not include

an offence committed in consequence of a contravention of subsection (1) of that section.
Commencement Information
I47. S. 30 in force at 23.11.2016 by S.I. 2016/1066, art. 2

31. Revocation of rent stopping orders

(1) A residential property tribunal may, in accordance with this section, revoke a rent stopping order made in respect of a dwelling under section 30.
(2) The tribunal may revoke an order only—
    (a) on an application by—
(i) the licensing authority for the area in which the dwelling is located,
(ii) the local housing authority for the area in which the dwelling is located, or
(iii) the landlord of the dwelling, and
    (b) if it is satisfied that an offence under section 7. (5) or 13. (3) is no longer being committed in relation to the dwelling.
(3) But a local housing authority may not make an application under subsection (2) without the consent of the licensing authority mentioned in paragraph (a)(i) of that subsection (unless it is the licensing authority); and consent for that purpose may be given generally or in respect of a particular application.
(4) Where the tribunal revokes a rent stopping order, periodical payments in connection with a domestic tenancy of the dwelling become payable from a date specified by the tribunal (which may, if the tribunal considers it appropriate, be a date earlier than the date on which the order is revoked).
(5) But revocation of a rent stopping order does not make a person liable to pay any periodical payments which, by virtue of the order, were stopped in respect of the period beginning with the stopping date (see section 30. (3)(a)) and ending with the date specified by the tribunal when revoking the order.
(6) If a rent stopping order is revoked following an application made under subsection (2)(a)(i) or (ii), the authority which made the application must notify the following persons that the order is revoked and of the effect of the revocation—
    (a) any tenant or occupier of the dwelling, and
    (b) the landlord of the dwelling.
(7) Where revocation occurs following an application made by a landlord, the licensing authority for the area in which the dwelling is located must ensure that any tenant or occupier of the dwelling is notified that the order is revoked and of the effect of the revocation.
(8) In subsection (2)(b)—
    (a) the reference to an offence section 7. (5) does not include an offence committed in consequence of a contravention of subsection (3) of that section, and
    (b) the reference to an offence committed under 13. (3) does not include an offence committed in consequence of a contravention of subsection (1) of that section.
Commencement Information
I48. S. 31 in force at 23.11.2016 by S.I. 2016/1066, art. 2

32. Rent repayment orders

(1) A residential property tribunal may, in accordance with this section and section 33, make an order (a "rent repayment order") in relation to a dwelling on an application made to it by—
    (a) the licensing authority for the area in which the dwelling is located,
    (b) the local housing authority for the area in which the dwelling is located, or
    (c) a tenant of the dwelling.
(2) But a local housing authority may not make an application under subsection (1) without the consent of the licensing authority mentioned in paragraph (a) of that subsection (unless it is the

licensing authority); and consent for that purpose may be given generally or in respect of a particular application.

(3) A "rent repayment order" is an order made in relation to a dwelling which requires the appropriate person (see subsection (9)) to pay to the applicant such amount in respect of the relevant award or awards of universal credit or the housing benefit paid as mentioned in subsection (5)(b), or (as the case may be) the periodical payments paid as mentioned in subsection (7)(b), as is specified in the order.

(4) The tribunal may make a rent repayment order only if it is satisfied—

(a) where the applicant is the licensing authority or a local housing authority (as the case may be), of the matters mentioned in subsection (5);

(b) where the applicant is a tenant, of the matters mentioned in subsection (7).

(5) The tribunal must be satisfied—

(a) that at any time within the period of 12 months ending with the date of the notice of intended proceedings required by subsection (6) an offence under section 7. (5) or 13. (3) has been committed in relation to the dwelling (whether or not a person has been charged or convicted for the offence);

(b) that—

(i) one or more relevant awards of universal credit have been paid (to any person), or

(ii) housing benefit has been paid (to any person) in respect of periodical payments payable in connection with a domestic tenancy of the dwelling,

during any period during which it appears to the tribunal that such an offence was being committed, and

(c) the requirements of subsection (6) have been complied with in relation to the application.

(6) Those requirements are—

(a) that the authority making the application must have given the appropriate person a notice (a "notice of intended proceedings")—

(i) informing the person that the authority is proposing to make an application for a rent repayment order,

(ii) setting out the reasons why it proposes to do so,

(iii) stating the amount that it will seek to recover under that subsection and how that amount is calculated, and

(iv) inviting the person to make representations to the authority within a period of not less than 28 days specified in the notice;

(b) that period must have expired, and

(c) that the authority must have considered any representations made to it within that period by the appropriate person.

(7) The tribunal must be satisfied that—

(a) a person has been convicted of an offence under section 7. (5) or 13. (3) in relation to the dwelling, or that a rent repayment order has required a person to make a payment in respect of—

(i) one or more relevant awards of universal credit, or

(ii) housing benefit paid in connection with a tenancy of the dwelling;

(b) the tenant paid to the appropriate person (whether directly or otherwise) periodical payments in respect of the tenancy of the dwelling during any period during which it appears to the tribunal that such an offence was being committed in relation to the dwelling, and

(c) the application is made within the period of 12 months beginning with—

(i) the date of the conviction or order, or

(ii) if such a conviction was followed by such an order (or vice versa), the date of the later of them.

(8) In this section—

(a) references to an offence under section 7. (5) do not include an offence committed in consequence of a contravention of subsection (3) of that section, and

(b) references to an offence committed under section 13. (3) do not include an offence committed in consequence of a contravention of subsection (1) of that section.

(9) In this section—
"appropriate person" ("person priodol"), in relation to any payment of universal credit or housing benefit or periodical payment in connection with a domestic tenancy of a dwelling, means the person who at the time of the payment was entitled to receive, on that person's own account, periodical payments in connection with the tenancy;
"housing benefit" ("budd-dal tai") means housing benefit provided by virtue of a scheme under section 123 of the Social Security Contributions and Benefits Act 1992;
"relevant award of universal credit" ("dyfarniad perthnasol o gredyd cynhwysol") means an award of universal credit the calculation of which included an amount under section 11 of the Welfare Reform Act 2012, calculated in accordance with Schedule 4 to the Universal Credit Regulations 2013 (housing costs element for renters) (SI 2013/376) or any corresponding provision replacing that Schedule, in respect of periodical payments in connection with a domestic tenancy of the dwelling;
"tenant" ("tenant"), in relation to any periodical payment, means a person who was a tenant at the time of the payment (and "tenancy" has a corresponding meaning).
(10) For the purposes of this section an amount which—
  (a) is not actually paid by a tenant but is used to discharge the whole or part of the tenant's liability in respect of a periodical payment (for example, by offsetting the amount against any such liability), and
  (b) is not an amount of universal credit or housing benefit,
is to be regarded as an amount paid by the tenant in respect of that periodical payment.
Commencement Information
I49. S. 32 in force at 23.11.2016 by S.I. 2016/1066, art. 2

33. Rent repayment orders: further provision

(1) Where, on an application by the licensing authority or a local housing authority (as the case may be) for a rent repayment order, the tribunal is satisfied—
  (a) that a person has been convicted of an offence under section 7. (5) or 13. (3) in relation to the dwelling to which the application relates, and
  (b) that—
(i) one or more relevant awards of universal credit were paid (whether or not to the appropriate person), or
(ii) housing benefit was paid (whether or not to the appropriate person) in respect of periodical payments payable in connection with a domestic tenancy of the dwelling during any period during which it appears to the tribunal that such an offence was being committed in relation to the dwelling in question,
the tribunal must make a rent repayment order requiring the appropriate person to pay to the authority which made the application the amount mentioned in subsection (2); but this is subject to subsections (3), (4) and (8).
(2) The amount is—
  (a) an amount equal to—
(i) where one relevant award of universal credit was paid as mentioned in subsection (1)(b)(i), the amount included in the calculation of that award under section 11 of the Welfare Reform Act 2012, calculated in accordance with Schedule 4 to the Universal Credit Regulations 2013 (housing costs element for renters) (SI 2013/376) or any corresponding provision replacing that Schedule, or the amount of the award if less, or
(ii) if more than one such award was paid as mentioned in subsection (1)(b)(i), the sum of the amounts included in the calculation of those awards as referred to in sub-paragraph (i), or the sum of the amounts of those awards if less, or
  (b) an amount equal to the total amount of housing benefit paid as mentioned in subsection (1)(b)(ii) (as the case may be).

(3) If the total of the amounts received by the appropriate person in respect of periodical payments payable as mentioned in paragraph (b) of subsection (1) ("the rent total") is less than the amount mentioned in subsection (2), the amount required to be paid by virtue of a rent repayment order made in accordance with subsection (1) is limited to the rent total.
(4) A rent repayment order made in accordance with subsection (1) may not require the payment of any amount which the tribunal is satisfied that, by reason of any exceptional circumstances, it would be unreasonable for that person to be required to pay.
(5) In a case where subsection (1) does not apply, the amount required to be paid by virtue of a rent repayment order is to be such amount as the tribunal considers reasonable in the circumstances; but this is subject to subsections (6) to (8).
(6) In such a case, the tribunal must take into account the following matters—
　(a) the total amount of relevant payments paid in connection with a tenancy of the dwelling during any period during which it appears to the tribunal that an offence was being committed in relation to the dwelling under section 7. (5) or 13. (3);
　(b) the extent to which that total amount—
(i) consisted of, or derived from, payments of relevant awards of universal credit or housing benefit, and
(ii) was actually received by the appropriate person;
　(c) whether the appropriate person has at any time been convicted of an offence under section 7. (5) or 13. (3);
　(d) the conduct and financial circumstances of the appropriate person; and
　(e) where the application is made by a tenant, the conduct of the tenant.
(7) In subsection (6) "relevant payments" means—
　(a) in relation to an application by the licensing authority or a local housing authority (as the case may be), payments of relevant awards of universal credit, housing benefit or periodical payments payable by tenants;
　(b) in relation to an application by a tenant, periodical payments payable by the tenant, less—
(i) where one or more relevant awards of universal credit were payable during the period in question, the amount mentioned in subsection (2)(a) in respect of the award or awards that related to the tenancy during that period, or
(ii) any amount of housing benefit payable in respect of the tenancy of the dwelling during the period in question.
(8) A rent repayment order may not require the payment of any amount which—
　(a) where the application is made by the licensing authority or a local housing authority (as the case may be), is in respect of any time falling outside the period of 12 months ending with the date of the notice of intended proceedings given under section 32. (6), or
　(b) where the application is made by a tenant, is in respect of any time falling outside the period of 12 months ending with the date of the tenant's application under section 32. (1);
and the period to be taken into account under subsection (6)(a) is restricted accordingly.
(9) Any amount payable by virtue of a rent repayment order is recoverable as a debt due to the licensing authority, local housing authority or tenant (as the case may be) from the appropriate person.
(10) And an amount payable to the licensing authority or a local housing authority by virtue of such an order does not, when recovered by it, constitute an amount of universal credit or housing benefit (as the case may be) recovered by the authority.
(11) Subsections (8), (9) and (10) of section 32 apply for the purposes of this section as they apply for the purposes of section 32.
Commencement Information
I50. S. 33 in force at 23.11.2016 by S.I. 2016/1066, art. 2

34. Power for Welsh Ministers to make regulations in relation to sections 32 and 33.

(1) The Welsh Ministers may by regulations make such provision as they consider appropriate for supplementing the provisions of sections 32 and 33.
(2) Regulations made under subsection (1) may, for example, make provision—
  (a) for securing that persons are not unfairly prejudiced by rent repayment orders (whether in cases where there have been over-payments of universal credit or housing benefit or otherwise);
  (b) requiring or authorising amounts received by the licensing authority or local housing authorities by virtue of rent repayment orders to be dealt with in such manner as is specified in the regulations.
Commencement Information
I51. S. 34 in force at 1.12.2014 for specified purposes by S.I. 2014/3127, art. 2. (b), Sch. Pt. 2
I52. S. 34 in force at 23.11.2016 in so far as not already in force by S.I. 2016/1066, art. 2

35. Offences by bodies corporate

(1) Where an offence under this Part committed by a body corporate is proved to have been committed with the consent or connivance of, or is attributable to any neglect on the part of—
  (a) a director, manager, or secretary of the body corporate, or
  (b) a person purporting to act in such a capacity,
that person as well as the body corporate commits the offence and is liable to be proceeded against and punished accordingly.
(2) The reference to the director, manager or secretary of the body corporate includes a reference—
  (a) to any similar officer of the body;
  (b) where the body is a body corporate whose affairs are managed by its members, to any officer or member of the body.
Commencement Information
I53. S. 35 in force at 23.11.2016 by S.I. 2016/1066, art. 2

Information

36. Requests for information from authorities and use of information by authorities

(1) If a licensing authority requests that a local housing authority provides it with information to which subsection (2) applies and which it requires for the purpose of exercising its functions under this Part, the local housing authority must comply with the request unless the local housing authority considers that doing so would—
  (a) be incompatible with the local housing authority's own duties, or
  (b) otherwise have an adverse effect on the exercise of the local housing authority's functions.
(2) This subsection applies to any information which has been obtained by a local housing authority in the exercise of its—
  (a) functions as the local housing authority;
  (b) functions under Part 1 of the Local Government Finance Act 1992 (council tax).
(3) Information obtained by a local housing authority under section 134 of the Social Security Administration Act 1992 (housing benefit) before the repeal of that section by Schedule 14 to the Welfare Reform Act 2012 is to be treated as information to which subsection (2) applies.
(4) If a licensing authority requests that another licensing authority provide it with information to which subsection (5) applies and which it requires for the purpose of exercising its functions under this Part, the other authority must comply with the request unless the other authority considers that

doing so would—
(a) be incompatible with its own duties, or
(b) otherwise have an adverse effect on the exercise of its functions.
(5) This subsection applies to any information which has been obtained by a licensing authority in the exercise of its functions under this Part.
(6) A licensing authority may use any information to which subsection (2) or (5) applies (whether or not obtained under subsection (1) or (4)) for any purpose connected with the exercise of the authority's functions under this Part.
(7) If a local housing authority requests that a licensing authority provide it with information to which subsection (5) applies and which it requires for the purpose of exercising its functions under this Part, the licensing authority must comply with the request unless the licensing authority considers that doing so would—
(a) be incompatible with its own duties, or
(b) otherwise have an adverse effect on the exercise of its functions.
(8) A local housing authority may use any information to which subsection (2) or (5) applies (whether or not obtained under (7)) for any purpose connected with the exercise of the authority's functions under this Part.
Commencement Information
I54. S. 36 in force at 23.11.2015 by S.I. 2015/1826, art. 2. (r)

37. Power to require documents to be produced or information given

(1) A person authorised in writing by a licensing authority may exercise the powers conferred by subsections (2) and (3) in relation to documents or information (as the case may be) reasonably required by the authority—
(a) for any purpose connected with the exercise of any of the authority's functions under this Part, or
(b) for the purpose of investigating whether any offence has been committed under this Part.
(2) A person authorised under subsection (1) may give a notice to a relevant person requiring that person—
(a) to produce any documents which—
(i) are specified or described in the notice, or fall within a category of document which is specified or described in the notice, and
(ii) are in the person's custody or under the person's control, and
(b) to produce them at a time and place, and to a person, specified in the notice.
(3) A person authorised under subsection (1) may give a notice to a relevant person requiring that person—
(a) to give any information which—
(i) is specified or described in the notice, or falls within a category of information which is specified or described in the notice, and
(ii) is known to the person, and
(b) to give it in a form and manner specified in the notice.
(4) The notice under subsection (2) or (3) must include information about the possible consequences of not complying with the notice.
(5) The person to whom any document is produced in accordance with a notice under subsection (2) or (3) may copy the document.
(6) No person may be required under this section to produce any document or give any information which the person would be entitled to refuse to provide in proceedings in the High Court on grounds of legal professional privilege.
(7) In this section "document" includes information recorded otherwise than in legible form, and in relation to information so recorded, any reference to the production of a document is a reference

to the production of a copy of the information in legible form.

(8) In this section "relevant person" means a person within any of the following paragraphs—

(a) a person who applies for a licence under this Part or who is the holder of a licence under this Part;

(b) a person who has an estate or interest in rental property;

(c) a person who is, or is proposing to be, involved in the letting or management of a rental property;

(d) a person who occupies a rental property.

Commencement Information

I55. S. 37 in force at 23.11.2015 by S.I. 2015/1826, art. 2. (s)

38. Enforcement of powers to obtain information

(1) A person who fails to do anything required of that person by a notice under section 37 commits an offence.

(2) In proceedings against a person for an offence under subsection (1) it is a defence that the person had a reasonable excuse for failing to comply with the notice.

(3) A person who commits an offence under subsection (1) is liable on summary conviction to a fine not exceeding level 4 on the standard scale.

(4) A person who intentionally alters, suppresses or destroys any document which the person has been required to produce by a notice under section 37 commits an offence.

(5) A person who commits an offence under subsection (4) is liable on summary conviction to a fine.

(6) In this section "document" includes information recorded otherwise than in legible form, and in relation to information so recorded—

(a) the reference to the production of a document is a reference to the production of a copy of the information in legible form, and

(b) the reference to suppressing a document includes a reference to destroying the means of reproducing the information.

Commencement Information

I56. S. 38 in force at 23.11.2015 by S.I. 2015/1826, art. 2. (t)

39. False or misleading information

(1) A person who—

(a) supplies any information to a licensing authority in connection with any of its functions under this Part which is false or misleading, and

(b) knows that it is false or misleading or is reckless as to whether it is false or misleading,

commits an offence.

(2) A person who—

(a) supplies any information to another person which is false or misleading,

(b) knows that it is false or misleading or is reckless as to whether it is false or misleading, and

(c) knows that the information is to be used for the purpose of supplying information to a licensing authority in connection with any of its functions under this Part,

commits an offence.

(3) A person who commits an offence under subsection (1) or (2) is liable on summary conviction to a fine.

(4) In this section "false or misleading" means false or misleading in any material respect.

Commencement Information

I57. S. 39 in force at 23.11.2015 by S.I. 2015/1826, art. 2. (u)

Powers of the Welsh Ministers

40. Code of practice

(1) The Welsh Ministers must issue a code of practice setting standards relating to letting and managing rental properties.
(2) Standards under subsection (1) may (among other things) be set in relation to training.
(3) The Welsh Ministers may—
    (a) issue a code of practice which, in part or in whole, applies only to specified persons or cases, or applies differently to different persons or cases;
    (b) amend or withdraw a code issued.
(4) Before issuing or amending a code of practice the Welsh Ministers must take reasonable steps to consult—
    (a) persons involved in letting and managing rental properties and persons occupying rental properties under a tenancy, or
    (b) persons whom the Welsh Ministers consider to represent the interests of the persons mentioned in paragraph (a),
on a draft of the code or a draft of an amended code ("the proposed code").
(5) If the Welsh Ministers wish to proceed with the proposed code (with or without modifications) they must lay a copy before the National Assembly for Wales.
(6) The Welsh Ministers must not issue the proposed code in the form of that draft unless it is approved by resolution of the National Assembly for Wales.
(7) Once approved the code or amended code comes into force on the date appointed by order of the Welsh Ministers.
(8) The Welsh Ministers may withdraw a code made under this section in an amended code or by direction.
(9) A code approved by the National Assembly for Wales may not be withdrawn unless a proposal to that effect is approved by resolution of the National Assembly.
(10) The Welsh Ministers must publish each code or amended code issued under this section.
Commencement Information
I58. S. 40 in force at 1.12.2014 for specified purposes by S.I. 2014/3127, art. 2. (c), Sch. Pt. 3
I59. S. 40 in force at 23.11.2016 in so far as not already in force by S.I. 2016/1066, art. 2

41. Guidance

(1) In exercising its functions under this Part, a licensing authority must have regard to any guidance given by the Welsh Ministers.
(2) In exercising functions under this Part other than as a licensing authority, a local housing authority must have regard to any guidance given by the Welsh Ministers.
(3) The Welsh Ministers may—
    (a) give guidance under this Part generally or to authorities of a specified description;
    (b) revise guidance given under this Part by giving further guidance;
    (c) revoke guidance given under this Part by giving further guidance or by notice.
(4) The Welsh Ministers must publish any guidance under this Part or notice under this section.
(5) Before giving, revising or revoking guidance under this Part, the Welsh Ministers must consult such persons as the Welsh Ministers consider appropriate.
(6) Consultation undertaken before the coming into force this section may satisfy the requirement in subsection (5).
Commencement Information
I60. S. 41 in force at 1.12.2014 for specified purposes by S.I. 2014/3127, art. 2. (c), Sch. Pt. 3

I61. S. 41 in force at 23.11.2016 in so far as not already in force by S.I. 2016/1066, art. 2

42. Directions

(1) In exercising its functions under this Part, a licensing authority must comply with any directions given by the Welsh Ministers.
(2) In exercising functions under this Part other than as a licensing authority, a local housing authority must comply with any directions given by the Welsh Ministers.
(3) A direction under subsection (2) may be given generally or to authorities of a specified description.
(4) A direction given under this section—
   (a) may be varied or revoked by a subsequent direction;
   (b) must be published.

Commencement Information
I62. S. 42 in force at 1.12.2014 for specified purposes by S.I. 2014/3127, art. 2. (b), Sch. Pt. 2
I63. S. 42 in force at 23.11.2016 in so far as not already in force by S.I. 2016/1066, art. 2

Supplementary

43. Activity in contravention of this Part: effect on tenancy agreements

(1) No rule of law relating to the validity or enforceability of contracts in circumstances involving illegality is to affect the validity or enforceability of any provision of a domestic tenancy of a dwelling in respect of which a contravention of this Part has occurred.
(2) But periodical payments—
   (a) payable in connection with such a tenancy may be stopped in accordance with section 30 (rent stopping orders), and
   (b) paid in connection with such a tenancy may be recovered in accordance with sections 32 and 33 (rent repayment orders).

Commencement Information
I64. S. 43 in force at 23.11.2016 by S.I. 2016/1066, art. 2

44. Restriction on terminating tenancies

(1) A section 21 notice may not be given in relation to a dwelling subject to a domestic tenancy which is an assured shorthold tenancy if—
   (a) the landlord is not registered in respect of the dwelling, or
   (b) the landlord is not licensed under this Part for the area in which the dwelling is located and the landlord has not appointed a person who is licensed under this Part to carry out all property management work in respect of the dwelling on the landlord's behalf.
(2) But subsection (1) does not apply for the period of 28 days beginning with the day on which the landlord's interest in the dwelling is assigned to the landlord.
(3) In this section, a "section 21 notice" means a notice under section 21. (1)(b) or (4)(a) of the Housing Act 1988.

Commencement Information
I65. S. 44 in force at 23.11.2016 by S.I. 2016/1066, art. 2

45. Landlords who are trustees

If trustees constitute a landlord, the landlord may be registered or licensed for the purposes of this Part under a name which is a collective description of the trustees as the trustees of the trust in question.
Commencement Information
I66. S. 45 in force at 23.11.2015 by S.I. 2015/1826, art. 2. (v)

46. Regulations about fees

(1) Regulations made under this Part which prescribe the amount of a fee payable by a person in connection with applications to be registered or licensed may provide that the fee is to be—
    (a) an amount stated in the regulations;
    (b) determined by a person or means specified in the regulations.
(2) Such regulations may prescribe a different fee for different persons.
Commencement Information
I67. S. 46 in force at 1.12.2014 for specified purposes by S.I. 2014/3127, art. 2. (b), Sch. Pt. 2
I68. S. 46 in force at 23.11.2016 in so far as not already in force by S.I. 2016/1066, art. 2

47. Information about applications

A licensing authority must publish information about its requirements relating to—
    (a) the form and content of applications to be registered and licensed;
    (b) information to be provided when making applications.
Commencement Information
I69. S. 47 in force at 23.11.2015 by S.I. 2015/1826, art. 2. (w)

48. Giving notification etc. under this Part

(1) This section applies where a provision of this Part requires or authorises (in whatever terms) a relevant person to—
    (a) notify a person of something, or
    (b) give a document to a person (including a notice or a copy of a document).
(2) The notification or document may be given to the person in question—
    (a) by delivering it to the person,
    (b) by sending it by post to the person's proper address,
    (c) by leaving it at the person's proper address, or
    (d) if the conditions in subsection (4) are met, by sending it electronically.
(3) The notification or document may be given to a body corporate by being given to the secretary or clerk of that body.
(4) A relevant person may send a notification or document to a person electronically only if the following requirements are met—
    (a) the person to whom the notification or document is to be given must have—
(i) indicated to the relevant person a willingness to receive the notification or document electronically, and
(ii) provided the relevant person with an address suitable for that purpose, and
    (b) the relevant person must send the notification or document to that address.
(5) For the purposes of this section and section 7 of the Interpretation Act 1978 (references to service by post) in its application to this section, the proper address of a person is—
    (a) in the case of a body corporate, the address of the registered or principal office of the body;
    (b) in any other case, the last known address of the person.
(6) A notification or document given to a person by leaving it at the person's proper address is to

be treated for the purposes of this Part as having been given at the time at which it was left at that address.

(7) Each of the following is a "relevant person" for the purposes of this section—

(a) a licensing authority;

(b) a local housing authority exercising functions under this Part other than as a licensing authority;

(c) a person who, by virtue of a written authorisation, exercises functions under this Part on behalf of a licensing authority or a local housing authority of the kind mentioned in paragraph (b).

Commencement Information

170. S. 48 in force at 23.11.2015 by S.I. 2015/1826, art. 2. (x)

General

49. Interpretation of this Part and index of defined terms

(1) In this Part—

"domestic tenancy" ("tenantiaeth ddomestig") has the meaning given by section 2;

"dwelling" ("annedd") has the meaning given by section 2;

"fully mutual housing association" ("cymdeithas dai cwbl gydfuddiannol") has the meaning given by section 1. (2) of the Housing Association Act 1985;

"landlord" ("landlord") has the meaning given by section 2;

"lettings work" ("gwaith gosod") has the meaning given by section 10;

"licensing authority" ("awdurdod trwyddedu") means a person designated by order under section 3;

"periodical payments" ("taliadau cyfnodol") means payments by way of rent or service charge;

"prescribed" ("rhagnodedig") means prescribed in regulations made by the Welsh Ministers;

"property management work" ("gwaith rheoli eiddo") has the meaning given by section 12;

"registered social landlord" ("landlord cymdeithasol cofrestredig") means a social landlord registered under Part 1 of the Housing Act 1996;

"rental property" ("eiddo ar rent") has the meaning given by section 2.

(2) In this Part, a reference to assignment of an interest to a landlord—

(a) includes any conveyance other than a mortgage or charge, and

(b) if trustees constitute the landlord, does not include a change in the persons who are for the time being the trustees of the trust.

(3) In this Part—

(a) any reference to an application for a licence includes a reference to an application for renewal of a licence, and

(b) any reference to the grant of a licence by a licensing authority includes a reference to renewal of a licence;

and related expressions are to be construed accordingly.

Commencement Information

171. S. 49 in force at 1.12.2014 for specified purposes by S.I. 2014/3127, art. 2. (b), Sch. Pt. 2

172. S. 49 in force at 23.11.2015 in so far as not already in force by S.I. 2015/1826, art. 2. (y)

Interpretation of this Part and index of defined terms

49. Interpretation of this Part and index of defined terms

(1) In this Part—
"domestic tenancy" ("tenantiaeth ddomestig") has the meaning given by section 2;
"dwelling" ("annedd") has the meaning given by section 2;
"fully mutual housing association" ("cymdeithas dai cwbl gydfuddiannol") has the meaning given by section 1. (2) of the Housing Association Act 1985;
"landlord" ("landlord") has the meaning given by section 2;
"lettings work" ("gwaith gosod") has the meaning given by section 10;
"licensing authority" ("awdurdod trwyddedu") means a person designated by order under section 3;
"periodical payments" ("taliadau cyfnodol") means payments by way of rent or service charge;
"prescribed" ("rhagnodedig") means prescribed in regulations made by the Welsh Ministers;
"property management work" ("gwaith rheoli eiddo") has the meaning given by section 12;
"registered social landlord" ("landlord cymdeithasol cofrestredig") means a social landlord registered under Part 1 of the Housing Act 1996;
"rental property" ("eiddo ar rent") has the meaning given by section 2.
(2) In this Part, a reference to assignment of an interest to a landlord—
   (a) includes any conveyance other than a mortgage or charge, and
   (b) if trustees constitute the landlord, does not include a change in the persons who are for the time being the trustees of the trust.
(3) In this Part—
   (a) any reference to an application for a licence includes a reference to an application for renewal of a licence, and
   (b) any reference to the grant of a licence by a licensing authority includes a reference to renewal of a licence;
and related expressions are to be construed accordingly.
Commencement Information
I1. S. 49 in force at 1.12.2014 for specified purposes by S.I. 2014/3127, art. 2. (b), Sch. Pt. 2
I2. S. 49 in force at 23.11.2015 in so far as not already in force by S.I. 2015/1826, art. 2. (y)

PART 2. HOMELESSNESS

PART 2 HOMELESSNESS

CHAPTER 1. HOMELESSNESS REVIEWS AND STRATEGIES

50. Duty to carry out a homelessness review and formulate a homelessness strategy

(1) A local housing authority must (periodically, as required by this section)—
   (a) carry out a homelessness review for its area, and
   (b) formulate and adopt a homelessness strategy based on the results of that review.
(2) The authority must adopt a homelessness strategy in 2018 and a new homelessness strategy in every fourth year after 2018.
(3) The Welsh Ministers may amend subsection (2) by order.
(4) A council of a county or county borough in Wales must take its homelessness strategy into account in the exercise of its functions (including functions other than its functions as local

housing authority).
(5) Nothing in subsection (4) affects any duty or requirement arising apart from this section.
(6) In this Chapter "homeless" has the meaning given by section 55 and "homelessness" is to be interpreted accordingly.
Commencement Information
I1. S. 50 in force at 1.12.2014 for specified purposes by S.I. 2014/3127, art. 2. (b), Sch. Pt. 2
I2. S. 50 in force at 27.4.2015 in so far as not already in force by S.I. 2015/1272, art. 2, Sch. para. 1

51. Homelessness reviews

(1) A homelessness review under section 50 must include a review of—
    (a) the levels, and likely future levels, of homelessness in the local housing authority's area;
    (b) the activities which are carried out in the local housing authority's area for the achievement of the following objectives (or which contribute to their achievement)—
(i) the prevention of homelessness;
(ii) that suitable accommodation is or will be available for people who are or may become homeless;
(iii) that satisfactory support is available for people who are or may become homeless;
    (c) the resources available to the authority (including the resources available in exercise of functions other than its functions as local housing authority), other public authorities, voluntary organisations and other persons for such activities.
(2) After completing a homelessness review, a local housing authority must publish the results of the review by—
    (a) making the results of the review available on its website (if it has one);
    (b) making a copy of the results of the review available at its principal office for inspection at all reasonable hours, without charge, by members of the public;
    (c) providing (on payment if required by the authority of a reasonable charge) a copy of those results to any member of the public who asks for one.
Commencement Information
I3. S. 51 in force at 27.4.2015 by S.I. 2015/1272, art. 2, Sch. para. 2

52. Homelessness strategies

(1) A homelessness strategy under section 50 is a strategy for achieving the following objectives in the local housing authority's area—
    (a) the prevention of homelessness;
    (b) that suitable accommodation is and will be available for people who are or may become homeless;
    (c) that satisfactory support is available for people who are or may become homeless.
(2) A homelessness strategy may specify more detailed objectives to be pursued, and action planned to be taken, in the exercise of any functions of the authority (including functions other than its functions as local housing authority).
(3) A homelessness strategy may also include provision relating to specific action which the authority expects to be taken—
    (a) by any public authority with functions which are capable of contributing to the achievement of any of the objectives mentioned in subsection (1), or
    (b) by any voluntary organisation or other person whose activities are capable of contributing to the achievement of any of those objectives.
(4) The inclusion in a homelessness strategy of any provision relating to action mentioned in subsection (3) requires the approval of the body or person concerned.
(5) In formulating a homelessness strategy the authority must consider (among other things) the

extent to which any of the objectives mentioned in subsection (1) can be achieved through action involving two or more of the bodies or other persons mentioned in subsections (2) and (3).
(6) A homelessness strategy must include provision relating to action planned by the authority to be taken in the exercise of its functions, and specific action expected by the authority to be taken by public authorities, voluntary organisations and other persons within subsection (3), in relation to those who may be in particular need of support if they are or may become homeless, including in particular—
 (a) people leaving prison or youth detention accommodation,
 (b) young people leaving care,
 (c) people leaving the regular armed forces of the Crown,
 (d) people leaving hospital after medical treatment for mental disorder as an inpatient, and
 (e) people receiving mental health services in the community.
(7) A local housing authority must keep its homelessness strategy under review and may modify it.
(8) Before adopting or modifying a homelessness strategy a local housing authority must consult such public or local authorities, voluntary organisations or other persons as it considers appropriate.
(9) After adopting or modifying a homelessness strategy, a local housing authority must publish the strategy by—
 (a) making a copy of the strategy available on its website (if it has one);
 (b) making a copy of the strategy available at its principal office for inspection at all reasonable hours, without charge, by members of the public;
 (c) providing (on payment if required by the authority of a reasonable charge) a copy of the strategy to any member of the public who asks for one.
(10) If the authority modifies its homelessness strategy, it may publish the modifications or the strategy as modified (as it considers most appropriate).
(11) Where the authority decides to publish only the modifications, the references to the homelessness strategy in paragraphs (a) to (c) of subsection (9) are to be interpreted as references to the modifications.
Commencement Information
I4. S. 52 in force at 27.4.2015 by S.I. 2015/1272, art. 2, Sch. para. 3

CHAPTER 2. HELP FOR PEOPLE WHO ARE HOMELESS OR THREATENED WITH HOMELESSNESS

53. Overview of this Chapter
(1) This Chapter confers duties on local housing authorities to help people who are homeless or threatened with homelessness and makes connected provision.
(2) Sections 55 to 59 define and otherwise explain the meaning of some key terms (further provision about interpretation and an index of terms defined in this Chapter is at section 99).
(3) Section 60 requires local housing authorities to secure the provision of a service providing people with information and advice connected with homelessness and assistance in accessing help under this Chapter.
(4) Section 61 introduces Schedule 2 which makes provision about eligibility for help under this Chapter.
(5) Section 62 places a duty on a local housing authority to assess the cases of people ("applicants") who apply to the authority for accommodation, or help in retaining or obtaining accommodation, where they appear to the authority to be homeless or threatened with homelessness.
(6) Section 63 provides for notice to be given to applicants about the outcome of the assessment.
(7) Section 64 gives examples of the kinds of ways in which the subsequent duties to secure or help to secure the availability of accommodation may be discharged and what may be done to

discharge them; and section 65 explains what "help to secure" means.

(8) Sections 66 to 79 set out the main duties on local housing authorities to help applicants, the circumstances in which those duties come to an end and connected provision; the main duties are—

   (a) a duty to help to prevent applicants who are threatened with homelessness from becoming homeless (section 66);

   (b) a duty to secure interim accommodation for applicants in priority need (section 68) (section 70 provides for who is to have priority need for accommodation for the purposes of the Chapter);

   (c) a duty to help to secure that suitable accommodation is available for occupation by homeless applicants (section 73);

   (d) a duty to secure accommodation for applicants in priority need when the duty in section 73 comes to an end (section 75).

(9) Section 78 provides for the circumstances in which local housing authorities may have regard to whether an applicant became homeless intentionally when it is considering whether a duty to secure accommodation for applicants in priority need applies; section 77 provides for the meaning of intentionally homeless.

(10) Sections 80 to 82 provide for local housing authorities to end their duties to applicants by referring their cases to other authorities in Wales or England, where the applicants have a local connection with the areas of those other authorities; section 81 defines the meaning of "local connection" for the purposes of this Chapter.

(11) Sections 85 to 89 provide for reviews and appeals.

(12) Sections 90 to 99 make supplementary and general provision.

Commencement Information

15. S. 53 in force at 27.4.2015 by S.I. 2015/1272, art. 2, Sch. para. 4

Key terms

54. Application of key terms

Sections 55 to 59 apply for the purposes of this Part.

Commencement Information

16. S. 54 in force at 27.4.2015 by S.I. 2015/1272, art. 2, Sch. para. 5

55. Meaning of homeless and threatened homelessness

(1) A person is homeless if there is no accommodation available for the person's occupation, in the United Kingdom or elsewhere, which the person—

   (a) is entitled to occupy by virtue of an interest in it or by virtue of an order of a court,

   (b) has an express or implied licence to occupy, or

   (c) occupies as a residence by virtue of any enactment or rule of law giving the person the right to remain in occupation or restricting the right of another person to recover possession.

(2) A person is also homeless if the person has accommodation but—

   (a) cannot secure entry to it, or

   (b) it consists of a moveable structure, vehicle or vessel designed or adapted for human habitation and there is no place where the person is entitled or permitted both to place it and to reside in it.

(3) A person is not to be treated as having accommodation unless it is accommodation which it would be reasonable for the person to continue to occupy.

(4) A person is threatened with homelessness if it is likely that the person will become homeless within 56 days.

Commencement Information

17. S. 55 in force at 27.4.2015 by S.I. 2015/1272, art. 2, Sch. para. 6

56. Meaning of accommodation available for occupation

(1) Accommodation may only be regarded as available for a person's occupation if it is available for occupation by that person together with—

(a) any other person who normally resides with that person as a member of his or her family, or

(b) any other person who might reasonably be expected to reside with that person.

(2) A reference in this Chapter to securing that accommodation is available for a person's occupation is to be interpreted accordingly.

Commencement Information

I8. S. 56 in force at 27.4.2015 by S.I. 2015/1272, art. 2, Sch. para. 7

57. Whether it is reasonable to continue to occupy accommodation

(1) It is not reasonable for a person to continue to occupy accommodation if it is probable that it will lead to the person, or a member of the person's household, being subjected to abuse.

(2) In this section "member of a person's household" means—

(a) a person who normally resides with him or her as member of his or her family, or

(b) any other person who might reasonably be expected to reside with that person.

(3) In determining whether it would be, or would have been, reasonable for a person to continue to occupy accommodation, a local housing authority—

(a) may have regard to the general circumstances prevailing in relation to housing in the area of the local housing authority to whom the person has applied for help in securing accommodation;

(b) must have regard to whether or not the accommodation is affordable for that person.

(4) The Welsh Ministers may by order specify—

(a) other circumstances in which it is to be regarded as reasonable or not reasonable for a person to continue to occupy accommodation, and

(b) other matters to be taken into account or disregarded in determining whether it would be, or would have been, reasonable for a person to continue to occupy accommodation.

Commencement Information

I9. S. 57 in force at 1.12.2014 for specified purposes by S.I. 2014/3127, art. 2. (b), Sch. Pt. 2

I10. S. 57 in force at 27.4.2015 in so far as not already in force by S.I. 2015/1272, art. 2, Sch. para. 8

58. Meaning of abuse and domestic abuse

(1) "Abuse" means physical violence, threatening or intimidating behaviour and any other form of abuse which, directly or indirectly, may give rise to the risk of harm; and abuse is "domestic abuse" where the victim is associated with the abuser.

(2) A person is associated with another person if—

(a) they are or have been married to each other;

(b) they are or have been civil partners of each other;

(c) they live or have lived together in an enduring family relationship (whether they are of different sexes or the same sex);

(d) they live or have lived in the same household;

(e) they are relatives;

(f) they have agreed to marry one another (whether or not that agreement has been terminated);

(g) they have entered into a civil partnership agreement between them (whether or not that agreement has been terminated);

(h) they have or have had an intimate personal relationship with each other which is or was of significant duration;

(i) in relation to a child, each of them is a parent of the child or has, or has had, parental responsibility for the child.

(3) If a child has been adopted or falls within subsection (4), two persons are also associated with each other for the purposes this Chapter if—

(a) one is a natural parent of the child or a parent of such a natural parent, and

(b) the other is—

(i) the child, or

(ii) a person who has become a parent of the child by virtue of an adoption order, who has applied for an adoption order or with whom the child has at any time been placed for adoption.

(4) A child falls within this section if—

(a) an adoption agency, within the meaning of section 2 of the Adoption and Children Act 2002, is authorised to place the child for adoption under section 19 of that Act (placing children with parental consent) or the child has become the subject of an order under section 21 of that Act (placement orders), or

(b) the child is freed for adoption by virtue of an order made—
(i) in England and Wales, under section 18 of the Adoption Act 1976,
(ii) in Northern Ireland, under Article 17. (1) or 18. (1) of the Adoption (Northern Ireland) Order 1987, or

(c) the child is the subject of a Scottish permanence order which includes granting authority to adopt.

(5) In this section—

"adoption order" ("gorchymyn mabwysiadu") means an adoption order within the meaning of section 72. (1) of the Adoption Act 1976 or section 46. (1) of the Adoption and Children Act 2002;

"civil partnership agreement" ("cytundeb partneriaeth sifil") has the meaning given by section 73 of the Civil Partnership Act 2004;

"parental responsibility" ("cyfrifoldeb rhiant") has the meaning given by section 3 of the Children Act 1989;

"relative" ("perthynas"), in relation to a person, means that person's parent, grandparent, child, grandchild, brother, half-brother, sister, half-sister, uncle, aunt, nephew, niece (including any person who is or has been in that relationship by virtue of a marriage or civil partnership or an enduring family relationship).

Commencement Information

I11. S. 58 in force at 27.4.2015 by S.I. 2015/1272, art. 2, Sch. para. 9

59. Suitability of accommodation

(1) In determining whether accommodation is suitable for a person, a local housing authority must have regard to the following enactments—

(a) Part 9 of the Housing Act 1985 (slum clearance);
(b) Part 10 of the Housing Act 1985 (overcrowding);
(c) Part 1 of the Housing Act 2004 (housing conditions);
(d) Part 2 of the Housing Act 2004 (licensing of houses in multiple occupation);
(e) Part 3 of the Housing Act 2004 (selective licensing of other residential accommodation);
(f) Part 4 of the Housing Act 2004 (additional control provisions in relation to residential accommodation);
(g) Part 1 of this Act (regulation of private rented housing).

(2) In determining whether accommodation is suitable for a person, a local housing authority must have regard to whether or not the accommodation is affordable for that person.

(3) The Welsh Ministers may by order specify—

(a) circumstances in which accommodation is or is not to be regarded as suitable for a person, and

(b) matters to be taken into account or disregarded in determining whether accommodation is suitable for a person.

Commencement Information

I12. S. 59 in force at 1.12.2014 for specified purposes by S.I. 2014/3127, art. 2. (b), Sch. Pt. 2
I13. S. 59 in force at 27.4.2015 in so far as not already in force by S.I. 2015/1272, art. 2, Sch. para. 10

Information, advice and assistance in accessing help

60. Duty to provide information, advice and assistance in accessing help

(1) A local housing authority must secure the provision, without charge, of a service providing people in its area, or people who have a local connection with its area, with—

(a) information and advice relating to preventing homelessness, securing accommodation when homeless, accessing any other help available for people who are homeless or may become homeless, and

(b) assistance in accessing help under this Chapter or any other help for people who are homeless or may become homeless.

(2) In relation to subsection (1)(a), the service must include, in particular, the publication of information and advice on the following matters—

(a) the system provided for by this Chapter and how the system operates in the authority's area;

(b) whether any other help for people who are homeless or may become homeless (whether or not the person is threatened with homelessness within the meaning of this Chapter) is available in the authority's area;

(c) how to access the help that is available.

(3) In relation to subsection (1)(b), the service must include, in particular, assistance in accessing help to prevent a person becoming homeless which is available whether or not the person is threatened with homelessness within the meaning of this Chapter.

(4) The local housing authority must, in particular by working with other public authorities, voluntary organisations and other persons, ensure that the service is designed to meet the needs of groups at particular risk of homelessness, including in particular—

(a) people leaving prison or youth detention accommodation,

(b) young people leaving care,

(c) people leaving the regular armed forces of the Crown,

(d) people leaving hospital after medical treatment for mental disorder as an inpatient, and

(e) people receiving mental health services in the community.

(5) Two or more local housing authorities may jointly secure the provision of a service under this section for their areas; and where they do so—

(a) references in this section to a local housing authority are to be read as references to the authorities acting jointly, and

(b) references in this section to a local housing authority's area are to be read as references to the combined area.

(6) The service required by this section may be integrated with the service required by section 17 of the Social Services and Well-being (Wales) Act 2014.

Commencement Information

I14. S. 60 in force at 27.4.2015 by S.I. 2015/1272, art. 2, Sch. para. 11

Eligibility

61. Eligibility for help under this Chapter

Schedule 2 has effect for the purposes of determining whether an applicant is eligible for help under the following provisions of this Chapter.

Commencement Information

I15. S. 61 in force at 27.4.2015 by S.I. 2015/1272, art. 2, Sch. para. 12 (with art. 5)

Applications for help and assessment

62. Duty to assess

(1) A local housing authority must carry out an assessment of a person's case if—

(a) the person has applied to a local housing authority for accommodation or help in retaining or obtaining accommodation,

(b) it appears to the authority that the person may be homeless or threatened with homelessness, and

(c) subsection (2) does not apply to the person.

(2) This subsection applies if the person has been assessed by a local housing authority under this section on a previous occasion and the authority is satisfied that—

(a) the person's circumstances have not changed materially since that assessment was carried out, and

(b) there is no new information that materially affects that assessment.

(3) In this Chapter, "applicant" means a person to whom the duty in subsection (1) applies.

(4) The authority must assess whether or not the applicant is eligible for help under this Chapter.

(5) If the applicant is eligible for help under this Chapter, the assessment must include an assessment of—

(a) the circumstances that have caused the applicant to be homeless or threatened with homelessness;

(b) the housing needs of the applicant and any person with whom the applicant lives or might reasonably be expected to live;

(c) the support needed for the applicant and any person with whom the applicant lives or might reasonably be expected to live to retain accommodation which is or may become available;

(d) whether or not the authority has any duty to the applicant under the following provisions of this Chapter.

(6) In carrying out an assessment, the local housing authority must—

(a) seek to identify the outcome the applicant wishes to achieve from the authority's help, and

(b) assess whether the exercise of any function under this Chapter could contribute to the achievement of that outcome.

(7) A local housing authority may carry out its assessment of the matters mentioned in subsections (5) and (6) before it has concluded that the applicant is eligible for help under this Chapter.

(8) A local housing authority must keep its assessment under review during the period in which the authority considers that it owes a duty to the applicant under the following provisions of this Chapter or that it may do so.

(9) A local housing authority must review its assessment in the following two cases—

Case 1 - where an applicant has been notified under section 63 that a duty is owed to the applicant under section 66 (duty to help to prevent an applicant from becoming homeless) and subsequently it appears to the authority that the duty under section 66 has or is likely to come to an end because the applicant is homeless;

Case 2 - where an applicant has been notified under section 63 that a duty is owed to the applicant under section 73 (duty to help to secure accommodation for homeless applicants) and subsequently it appears to the authority that the duty in section 73 has or is likely to come to an end in circumstances where a duty may be owed to the applicant under section 75 (duty to secure accommodation for applicants in priority need when the duty in section 73 ends).

(10) The duty in subsection (5)(d) does not require a local housing authority to assess whether or not a duty would be owed to the applicant under section 75 unless and until it reviews its assessment in accordance with subsection (9) in the circumstances described in case 2 of that subsection; but it may do so before then.

(11) Subsections (9) and (10) do not affect the generality of subsection (8).

Commencement Information

I16. S. 62 in force at 27.4.2015 by S.I. 2015/1272, art. 2, Sch. para. 13

63. Notice of the outcome of assessment

(1) The local housing authority must notify the applicant of the outcome of its assessment (or any review of its assessment) and, in so far as any issue is decided against the applicant's interests, inform the applicant of the reasons for its decision.

(2) If the authority decides that a duty is owed to the applicant under section 75, but would not have done so without having had regard to a restricted person, the notice under subsection (1) must also—

(a) inform the applicant that its decision was reached on that basis,

(b) include the name of the restricted person,

(c) explain why the person is a restricted person, and

(d) explain the effect of section 76. (5).

(3) If the authority has notified or intends to notify another local housing authority under section

80 (referral of cases), it must at the same time notify the applicant of that decision and inform him or her of the reasons for it.

(4) A notice under subsection (1) or (3) must also—

(a) inform the applicant of his or her right to request a review of the decision and of the time within which such a request must be made (see section 85), and

(b) be given in writing and, if not received, is to be treated as having been given if it is made available at the authority's office for a reasonable period for collection by the applicant or on the applicant's behalf.

(5) In this Chapter, "a restricted person" means a person—

(a) who is not eligible for help under this Chapter,

(b) who is subject to immigration control within the meaning of the Asylum and Immigration Act 1996, and

(c) who either—

(i) does not have leave to enter or remain in the United Kingdom, or

(ii) has leave to enter or remain in the United Kingdom subject to a condition to maintain and accommodate himself or herself, and any dependants, without recourse to public funds.

Commencement Information

I17. S. 63 in force at 27.4.2015 by S.I. 2015/1272, art. 2, Sch. para. 14

Duties to help applicants

64. How to secure or help to secure the availability of accommodation

(1) The following are examples of the ways in which a local housing authority may secure or help to secure that suitable accommodation is available, or does not cease to be available, for occupation by an applicant—

(a) by arranging for a person other than the authority to provide something;

(b) by itself providing something;

(c) by providing something, or arranging for something to be provided, to a person other than the applicant.

(2) The following are examples of what may be provided or arranged to secure or help to secure that suitable accommodation is available, or does not cease to be available, for occupation by an applicant—

(a) mediation;

(b) payments by way of grant or loan;

(c) guarantees that payments will be made;

(d) support in managing debt, mortgage arrears or rent arrears;

(e) security measures for applicants at risk of abuse;

(f) advocacy or other representation;

(g) accommodation;

(h) information and advice;

(i) other services, goods or facilities.

(3) The Welsh Ministers must give guidance to local housing authorities in relation to how they may secure or help to secure that suitable accommodation is available, or does not cease to be available, for occupation by an applicant.

Commencement Information

I18. S. 64 in force at 1.12.2014 for specified purposes by S.I. 2014/3127, art. 2. (c), Sch. Pt. 3

I19. S. 64 in force at 27.4.2015 in so far as not already in force by S.I. 2015/1272, art. 2, Sch. para. 15

65. Meaning of help to secure

Where a local housing authority is required by this Chapter to help to secure (rather than "to secure") that suitable accommodation is available, or does not cease to be available, for occupation by an applicant, the authority—

(a) is required to take reasonable steps to help, having regard (among other things) to the need to make the best use of the authority's resources;
(b) is not required to secure an offer of accommodation under Part 6 of the Housing Act 1996 (allocation of housing);
(c) is not required to otherwise provide accommodation.
Commencement Information
120. S. 65 in force at 27.4.2015 by S.I. 2015/1272, art. 2, Sch. para. 16
66. Duty to help to prevent an applicant from becoming homeless
(1) A local housing authority must help to secure that suitable accommodation does not cease to be available for occupation by an applicant if the authority is satisfied that the applicant is—
(a) threatened with homelessness, and
(b) eligible for help.
(2) Subsection (1) does not affect any right of the authority, whether by virtue of a contract, enactment or rule of law, to secure vacant possession of any accommodation.
Commencement Information
121. S. 66 in force at 27.4.2015 by S.I. 2015/1272, art. 2, Sch. para. 17
67. Circumstances in which the duty in section 66 ends
(1) The duty to an applicant under section 66 comes to an end in any of the circumstances described in subsection (2), (3) or (4), if the applicant has been notified in accordance with section 84.
(2) The circumstances are that the local authority is satisfied that the applicant has become homeless.
(3) The circumstances are that the local housing authority is satisfied (whether as a result of the steps it has taken or not) that—
(a) the applicant is no longer threatened with homelessness, and
(b) suitable accommodation is likely to be available for occupation by the applicant for a period of at least 6 months.
(4) The circumstances are that—
(a) the applicant, having been notified in writing of the possible consequences of refusal or acceptance of the offer, refuses an offer of accommodation from any person which the authority is satisfied is suitable for the applicant, and
(b) the authority is satisfied that the accommodation offered is likely to be available for occupation by the applicant for a period of at least 6 months.
(5) The period of 6 months mentioned in subsections (3)(b) and (4)(b) begins on the day the notice under section 84 is sent or first made available for collection.
(6) See section 79 for further circumstances in which the duty in section 66 comes to an end.
Commencement Information
122. S. 67 in force at 27.4.2015 by S.I. 2015/1272, art. 2, Sch. para. 18
68. Interim duty to secure accommodation for homeless applicants in priority need
(1) The local housing authority must secure that suitable accommodation is available for the occupation of an applicant to whom subsection (2) or (3) applies until the duty comes to an end in accordance with section 69.
(2) This subsection applies to an applicant who the authority has reason to believe may—
(a) be homeless,
(b) be eligible for help, and
(c) have a priority need for accommodation,
in circumstances where the authority is not yet satisfied that the applicant is homeless, eligible for help and in priority need for accommodation.
(3) This subsection applies to an applicant—
(a) who the authority has reason to believe or is satisfied has a priority need or whose case has been referred from a local housing authority in England under section 198. (1) of the Housing Act 1996, and
(b) to whom the duty in section 73 (duty to help to end homelessness) applies.

(4) The duty under this section arises irrespective of any possibility of the referral of the applicant's case to another local housing authority (see sections 80 to 82).
Commencement Information
I23. S. 68 in force at 27.4.2015 by S.I. 2015/1272, art. 2, Sch. para. 19

69. Circumstances in which the duty in section 68 ends

(1) The duty to an applicant under section 68 comes to an end in any of the circumstances described in subsection (2), (3) (subject to subsection (4) and (5)), (7), (8) or (9) if the applicant has been notified in accordance with section 84.
(2) The circumstances are that the local housing authority has decided that no duty is owed to the applicant under section 73 and the applicant is notified of that decision.
(3) In the case of an applicant to whom section 68. (3) applies, the circumstances are that the local housing authority has—
    (a) decided that the duty owed to the applicant under section 73 has come to an end and that a duty is or is not owed to the applicant under section 75, and
    (b) notified the applicant of that decision;
but this is subject to subsections (4) and (5).
(4) Subsection (5) applies where a local housing authority has decided that no duty is owed to the applicant under section 75 on the basis that the authority—
    (a) is satisfied that the applicant became homeless intentionally in the circumstances which gave rise to the application, or
    (b) has previously secured an offer of accommodation of the kind described in section 75. (3)(f).
(5) The duty under section 68 does not come to an end in the circumstances described in subsection (3) until the authority is also satisfied that the accommodation it has secured under section 68 has been available to the applicant for a sufficient period, beginning on the day on which he or she is notified that section 75 does not apply, to allow the applicant a reasonable opportunity of securing accommodation for his or her occupation.
(6) The period mentioned in subsection (5) is not sufficient for the purposes of that subsection if it ends on a day during the period of 56 days beginning with the day on which the applicant was notified that the duty in section 73 applied.
(7) The circumstances are that the applicant, having been notified of the possible consequence of refusal, refuses an offer of accommodation secured under section 68 which the local housing authority is satisfied is suitable for the applicant.
(8) The circumstances are that the local housing authority is satisfied that the applicant has become homeless intentionally from suitable interim accommodation made available for the applicant's occupation under section 68.
(9) The circumstances are that the local housing authority is satisfied that the applicant voluntarily ceased to occupy as his or her only or principal home suitable interim accommodation made available for the applicant's occupation under section 68.
(10) The duty comes to an end in accordance with this section even if the applicant requests a review of any decision that has led to the duty coming to an end (see section 85).
(11) The authority may secure that suitable accommodation is available for the applicant's occupation pending a decision on a review.
(12) See section 79 for further circumstances in which the duty in section 68 comes to an end.
Commencement Information
I24. S. 69 in force at 27.4.2015 by S.I. 2015/1272, art. 2, Sch. para. 20

70. Priority need for accommodation

(1) The following persons have a priority need for accommodation for the purposes of this Chapter—
    (a) a pregnant woman or a person with whom she resides or might reasonably be expected to reside;
    (b) a person with whom a dependent child resides or might reasonably be expected to reside;
    (c) a person—
(i) who is vulnerable as a result of some special reason (for example: old age, physical or mental

illness or physical or mental disability), or
(ii) with whom a person who falls within sub-paragraph (i) resides or might reasonably be expected to reside;
 (d) a person—
(i) who is homeless or threatened with homelessness as a result of an emergency such as flood, fire or other disaster, or
(ii) with whom a person who falls within sub-paragraph (i) resides or might reasonably be expected to reside;
 (e) a person—
(i) who is homeless as a result of being subject to domestic abuse, or
(ii) with whom a person who falls within sub-paragraph (i) resides (other than the abuser) or might reasonably be expected to reside;
 (f) a person—
(i) who is aged 16 or 17 when the person applies to a local housing authority for accommodation or help in obtaining or retaining accommodation, or
(ii) with whom a person who falls within sub-paragraph (i) resides or might reasonably be expected to reside;
 (g) a person—
(i) who has attained the age of 18, when the person applies to a local housing authority for accommodation or help in obtaining or retaining accommodation, but not the age of 21, who is at particular risk of sexual or financial exploitation, or
(ii) with whom a person who falls within sub-paragraph (i) resides (other than an exploiter or potential exploiter) or might reasonably be expected to reside;
 (h) a person—
(i) who has attained the age of 18, when the person applies to a local housing authority for accommodation or help in obtaining or retaining accommodation, but not the age of 21, who was looked after, accommodated or fostered at any time while under the age of 18, or
(ii) with whom a person who falls within sub-paragraph (i) resides or might reasonably be expected to reside;
 (i) a person—
(i) who has served in the regular armed forces of the Crown who has been homeless since leaving those forces, or
(ii) with whom a person who falls within sub-paragraph (i) resides or might reasonably be expected to reside;
 (j) a person who has a local connection with the area of the local housing authority and who is vulnerable as a result of one of the following reasons—
(i) having served a custodial sentence within the meaning of section 76 of the Powers of Criminal Courts (Sentencing) Act 2000,
(ii) having been remanded in or committed to custody by an order of a court, or
(iii) having been remanded to youth detention accommodation under section 91. (4) of the Legal Aid, Sentencing and Punishment of Offenders Act 2012,
or a person with whom such a person resides or might reasonably be expected to reside.
(2) In this Chapter—
"looked after, accommodated or fostered" ("yn derbyn gofal, yn cael ei letya neu'n cael ei faethu") means—
 - looked after by a local authority (within the meaning of section 74 of the Social Services and Well-Being (Wales) Act 2014 or section 22 of the Children Act 1989),
 - accommodated by or on behalf of a voluntary organisation,
 - accommodated in a private children's home,
 - accommodated for a continuous period of at least three months—
by any Local Health Board or Special Health Authority,
by or on behalf of a clinical commissioning group or the National Health Service Commissioning Board,

by or on behalf of a county or county borough council in Wales in the exercise of education functions,

by or on behalf of a local authority in England in the exercise of education functions,

in any care home or independent hospital, or

in any accommodation provided by or on behalf of an NHS Trust or by or on behalf of an NHS Foundation Trust, or

- privately fostered (within the meaning of section 66 of the Children Act 1989).

(3) In subsection (2)—

"care home" ("cartref gofal") has the same meaning as in the Care Standards Act 2000;

"clinical commissioning group" ("grŵp comisiynu clinigol") means a body established under section 14. D of the National Health Service Act 2006;

"education functions" ("swyddogaethau addysg") has the meaning given by section 597. (1) of the Education Act 1996;

"independent hospital" ("ysbyty annibynnol")—

- in relation to Wales, has the meaning given by section 2 of the Care Standards Act 2000, and
- in relation to England, means a hospital as defined by section 275 of the National Health Service Act 2006 that is not a health service hospital as defined by that section;

"local authority in England" ("awdurdod lleol yn Lloegr") means—

- a county council in England,
- a district council for an area in England for which there is no county council,
- a London borough council, or
- the Common Council of the City of London;

"Local Health Board" ("Bwrdd Iechyd Lleol") means a Local Health Board established under section 11 of the National Health Service (Wales) Act 2006.

Commencement Information

I25. S. 70 in force at 27.4.2015 by S.I. 2015/1272, art. 2, Sch. para. 21

71. Meaning of vulnerable in section 70.

(1) A person is vulnerable as a result of a reason mentioned in paragraph (c) or (j) of section 70.

(1) if, having regard to all the circumstances of the person's case—

(a) the person would be less able to fend for himself or herself (as a result of that reason) if the person were to become street homeless than would an ordinary homeless person who becomes street homeless, and

(b) this would lead to the person suffering more harm than would be suffered by the ordinary homeless person;

this subsection applies regardless of whether or not the person whose case is being considered is, or is likely to become, street homeless.

(2) In subsection (1), "street homeless" ("digartref ac ar y stryd"), in relation to a person, means that the person has no accommodation available for the person's occupation in the United Kingdom or elsewhere, which the person—

(a) is entitled to occupy by virtue of an interest in it or by virtue of an order of a court,

(b) has an express or implied licence to occupy, or

(c) occupies as a residence by virtue of any enactment or rule of law giving the person the right to remain in occupation or restricting the right of another person to recover possession;

and sections 55 and 56 do not apply to this definition.

Commencement Information

I26. S. 71 in force at 27.4.2015 by S.I. 2015/1272, art. 2, Sch. para. 22

72. Power to amend or repeal provisions about priority need for accommodation

(1) The Welsh Ministers may by order—

(a) make provision for and in connection with removing any condition that a local housing authority must have reason to believe or be satisfied that an applicant is in priority need for accommodation before any power or duty to secure accommodation under this Chapter applies;

(b) amend or omit the descriptions of persons as having a priority need for accommodation for the purposes of this Chapter;

(c) specify further descriptions of persons as having a priority need for accommodation for the purposes of this Chapter.

(2) An order under subsection (1) may amend or repeal any provision of this Part.

(3) Before making an order under this section the Welsh Ministers must consult such associations representing councils of counties and county boroughs in Wales, and such other persons, as they consider appropriate.

Commencement Information

127. S. 72 in force at 1.12.2014 for specified purposes by S.I. 2014/3127, art. 2. (b), Sch. Pt. 2

128. S. 72 in force at 27.4.2015 in so far as not already in force by S.I. 2015/1272, art. 2, Sch. para. 23

73. Duty to help to secure accommodation for homeless applicants

(1) A local housing authority must help to secure that suitable accommodation is available for occupation by an applicant, if the authority is satisfied that the applicant is—

(a) homeless, and

(b) eligible for help.

(2) But the duty in subsection (1) does not apply if the authority refers the application to another local housing authority (see section 80).

Commencement Information

129. S. 73 in force at 27.4.2015 by S.I. 2015/1272, art. 2, Sch. para. 24

74. Circumstances in which the duty in section 73 ends

(1) The duty to an applicant under section 73 comes to an end in any of the circumstances described in subsections (2), (3), (4), or (5), if the applicant has been notified in accordance with section 84.

(2) The circumstances are the end of a period of 56 days.

(3) The circumstances are that before the end of a period of 56 days the local housing authority is satisfied that reasonable steps have been taken to help to secure that suitable accommodation is available for occupation by the applicant.

(4) The circumstances are that the local housing authority is satisfied (whether as a result of the steps it has taken or not) that—

(a) the applicant has suitable accommodation available for occupation, and

(b) the accommodation is likely to be available for occupation by the applicant for a period of at least 6 months.

(5) The circumstances are that—

(a) the applicant, having been notified of the possible consequence of refusal or acceptance of the offer, refuses an offer of accommodation from any person which the authority is satisfied is suitable for the applicant, and

(b) the authority is satisfied that the accommodation offered is likely to be available for occupation by the applicant for a period of at least 6 months.

(6) The period of 56 days mentioned in subsections (2) and (3) begins on the day the applicant is notified under section 63 and for this purpose the applicant is to be treated as notified on the day the notice is sent or first made available for collection.

(7) The period of 6 months mentioned in subsection (4)(b) and (5)(b) begins on the day the notice under section 84 is sent or first made available for collection.

(8) See section 79 for further circumstances in which the duty in section 73 comes to an end.

Commencement Information

130. S. 74 in force at 27.4.2015 by S.I. 2015/1272, art. 2, Sch. para. 25

75. Duty to secure accommodation for applicants in priority need when the duty in section 73 ends

(1) When the duty in section 73 (duty to help to secure accommodation for homeless applicants) comes to an end in respect of an applicant in the circumstances mentioned in subsection (2) o r (3) of section 74, the local housing authority must secure that suitable accommodation is available for occupation by the applicant if subsection (2) or (3) (of this section) applies.

(2) This subsection applies where the local housing authority—

(a) is satisfied that the applicant—

(i) does not have suitable accommodation available for occupation, or
(ii) has suitable accommodation, but it is not likely that the accommodation will be available for occupation by the applicant for a period of at least 6 months starting on the day the applicant is notified in accordance with section 84 that section 73 does not apply,
  (b) is satisfied that the applicant is eligible for help,
  (c) is satisfied that the applicant has a priority need for accommodation, and
  (d) if the authority is having regard to whether or not the applicant is homeless intentionally (see section 77), is not satisfied that the applicant became homeless intentionally in the circumstances which gave rise to the application;
(3) This subsection applies where the local housing authority is having regard to whether or not the applicant is homeless intentionally and is satisfied that—
  (a) the applicant became homeless intentionally in the circumstances which gave rise to the application,
  (b) the applicant—
(i) does not have suitable accommodation available for occupation, or
(ii) has suitable accommodation, but it is not likely that the accommodation will be available for occupation by the applicant for a period of at least 6 months starting on the day on which the applicant is notified in accordance with section 84 that section 73 does not apply,
  (c) the applicant is eligible for help,
  (d) the applicant has a priority need for accommodation,
  (e) the applicant is—
(i) a pregnant woman or a person with whom she resides or might reasonably be expected to reside,
(ii) a person with whom a dependent child resides or might reasonably be expected to reside,
(iii) a person who had not attained the age of 21 when the application for help was made or a person with whom such a person resides or might reasonably be expected to reside, or
(iv) a person who had attained the age of 21, but not the age of 25, when the application for help was made and who was looked after, accommodated or fostered at any time while under the age of 18, or a person with whom such a person resides or might reasonably be expected to reside, and
  (f) the authority has not previously secured an offer of accommodation to the applicant under this section following a previous application for help under this Chapter, where that offer was made—
(i) at any time within the period of 5 years before the day on which the applicant was notified under section 63 that a duty was owed to him or her under this section, and
(ii) on the basis that the applicant fell within this subsection.
(4) For the purpose of subsections (2)(a)(ii) and (3)(b)(ii), the applicant is to be treated as notified on the day the notice is sent or first made available for collection.
Commencement Information
I31. S. 75. (1)(2)(4) in force at 27.4.2015 by S.I. 2015/1272, art. 2, Sch. para. 26 (with art. 6)
76. Circumstances in which the duty in section 75 ends
(1) The duty to an applicant under section 75. (1) comes to an end in any of the circumstances described in subsections (2), (3), (6) or (7), if the applicant has been notified in accordance with section 84.
(2) The circumstances are that the applicant accepts—
  (a) an offer of suitable accommodation under Part 6 of the Housing Act 1996 (allocation of housing), or
  (b) an offer of suitable accommodation under an assured tenancy (including an assured shorthold tenancy).
(3) The circumstances are that the applicant, having been given notice in writing of the possible consequence of refusal or acceptance of the offer, refuses—
  (a) an offer of suitable interim accommodation under section 75,
  (b) a private rented sector offer, or
  (c) an offer of accommodation under Part 6 of the Housing Act 1996,

which the authority is satisfied is suitable for the applicant.

(4) For the purposes of this section an offer is a private rented sector offer if—

(a) it is an offer of an assured shorthold tenancy made by a private landlord to the applicant in relation to any accommodation which is available for the applicant's occupation,

(b) it is made, with the approval of the authority, in pursuance of arrangements made by the authority with the landlord with a view to bringing the authority's duty under section 75 to an end, and

(c) the tenancy being offered is a fixed term tenancy for a period of at least 6 months.

(5) In a restricted case, the local housing authority must, so far as reasonably practicable, bring its duty to an end by securing a private rented sector offer; for this purpose, a "restricted case" means a case where the local housing authority would not be satisfied as mentioned in section 75. (1) without having regard to a restricted person (see section 63. (5)).

(6) The circumstances are that the local housing authority is satisfied that the applicant has become homeless intentionally from suitable interim accommodation made available for the applicant's occupation—

(a) under section 68 and which continues to be made available under section 75, or

(b) under section 75.

(7) The circumstances are that the local housing authority is satisfied that the applicant has voluntarily ceased to occupy as his or her only or principal home, suitable interim accommodation made available for the applicant's occupation—

(a) under section 68 and which continues to be made available under section 75, or

(b) under section 75.

(8) See section 79 for further circumstances in which the duty in section 75. (1) comes to an end.

(9) In this section "fixed term tenancy" has the meaning given by Part 1 of the Housing Act 1988.

Commencement Information

I32. S. 76 in force at 27.4.2015 by S.I. 2015/1272, art. 2, Sch. para. 27

77. Meaning of intentionally homeless

(1) A person is intentionally homeless for the purpose of this Chapter if subsection (2) or (4) apply.

(2) This subsection applies if the person deliberately does or fails to do anything in consequence of which the person ceases to occupy accommodation which is available for the person's occupation and which it would have been reasonable for the person to continue to occupy.

(3) For the purposes of subsection (2) an act or omission in good faith on the part of a person who was unaware of any relevant fact may not be treated as deliberate.

(4) This subsection applies if—

(a) the person enters into an arrangement under which the person is required to cease to occupy accommodation which it would have been reasonable for the person to continue to occupy, and

(b) the purpose of the arrangement is to enable the person to become entitled to help under this Chapter,

and there is no other good reason why the person is homeless.

Commencement Information

I33. S. 77 in force at 27.4.2015 by S.I. 2015/1272, art. 2, Sch. para. 28

78. Deciding to have regard to intentionality

(1) The Welsh Ministers must, by regulations, specify a category or categories of applicant for the purpose of this section.

(2) A local housing authority may not have regard to whether or not an applicant has become homeless intentionally for the purposes of sections 68 and 75 unless—

(a) the applicant falls within a category specified under subsection (1) in respect of which the authority has decided to have regard to whether or not applicants in that category have become homeless intentionally, and

(b) the authority has published a notice of its decision under paragraph (a) which specifies the category.

(3) Subsection (4) applies where a local housing authority has published a notice under subsection

(2) unless the authority has—
    (a) decided to stop having regard to whether or not applicants falling into the category specified in the notice have become homeless intentionally, and
    (b) published a notice of its decision specifying the category.
(4) For the purposes of section 68 and 75, a local housing authority must have regard to whether or not an applicant has become homeless intentionally if the applicant falls within a category specified in the notice published by the authority under subsection (2).
Commencement Information
I34. S. 78 in force at 1.12.2014 for specified purposes by S.I. 2014/3127, art. 2. (b), Sch. Pt. 2
I35. S. 78 in force at 1.7.2015 in so far as not already in force by S.I. 2015/1272, art. 3 (with art. 7)
I36. S. 78. (2) in force at 27.4.2015 for specified purposes by S.I. 2015/1272, art. 2, Sch. para. 29
79. Further circumstances in which the duties to help applicants end
(1) The duties in sections 66, 68, 73 and 75 come to an end in the circumstances described in subsection (2), (3), (4) or (5), if the applicant is notified in accordance with section 84.
(2) The circumstances are that the local housing authority is no longer satisfied that the applicant is eligible for help.
(3) The circumstances are that the local housing authority is satisfied that a mistake of fact led to the applicant being notified under section 63 that the duty was owed to the applicant.
(4) The circumstances are that the local authority is satisfied that the applicant has withdrawn his or her application.
(5) The circumstances are that the local housing authority is satisfied that the applicant is unreasonably failing to co-operate with the authority in connection with the exercise of its functions under this Chapter as they apply to the applicant.
Commencement Information
I37. S. 79 in force at 27.4.2015 by S.I. 2015/1272, art. 2, Sch. para. 30

Referral to another local housing authority

80. Referral of case to another local housing authority
(1) Subsection (2) applies where—
    (a) a local housing authority considers that the conditions for referral to another local housing authority (whether in Wales or England) are met (see subsection (3)), and
    (b) the local housing authority would, if the case is not referred, be subject to the duty in section 73 in respect of an applicant who is in priority need of accommodation and unintentionally homeless (duty to help to secure accommodation for homeless applicants).
(2) The local housing authority may notify the other authority of its opinion that the conditions for referral are met in respect of the applicant.
(3) The conditions for referral of the case to another local housing authority (whether in Wales or England) are met if—
    (a) neither the applicant nor any person who might reasonably be expected to reside with the applicant has a local connection with the area of the authority to which the application was made,
    (b) the applicant or a person who might reasonably be expected to reside with the applicant has a local connection with the area of that other authority, and
    (c) neither the applicant nor any person who might reasonably be expected to reside with the applicant will run the risk of domestic abuse in that other area.
(4) But the conditions for referral mentioned in subsection (3) are not met if—
    (a) the applicant or any person who might reasonably be expected to reside with the applicant has suffered abuse (other than domestic abuse) in the area of the other authority, and
    (b) it is probable that the return to that area of the victim will lead to further abuse of a similar kind against him or her.
(5) The question of whether the conditions for referral of a case are satisfied is to be decided—
    (a) by agreement between the notifying authority and the notified authority, or

(b) in default of agreement, in accordance with such arrangements—
(i) as the Welsh Ministers may direct by order, where both authorities are in Wales, or
(ii) as the Welsh Ministers and the Secretary of State may jointly direct by order, where the notifying authority is in Wales and the notified authority is in England.
(6) An order under subsection (5) may direct that the arrangements are to be—
    (a) those agreed by any relevant authorities or associations of relevant authorities, or
    (b) in default of such agreement, such arrangements as appear to the Welsh Ministers or, in the case of an order under subsection (5)(b)(ii), to the Welsh Ministers and the Secretary of State to be suitable, after consultation with such associations representing relevant authorities, and such other persons, as they think appropriate.
(7) In subsection (6), "relevant authority" means a local housing authority or a social services authority; and it includes, in so far as that subsection applies to arrangements under subsection (5)(b)(ii), such authorities in Wales and England.
(8) The Welsh Ministers may by order specify other circumstances in which the conditions are or are not met for referral of the case to another local housing authority.

Commencement Information

138. S. 80 in force at 1.12.2014 for specified purposes by S.I. 2014/3127, art. 2. (b), Sch. Pt. 2
139. S. 80 in force at 27.4.2015 in so far as not already in force by S.I. 2015/1272, art. 2, Sch. para. 31

81. Local connection

(1) This section applies for the purposes of this Chapter.
(2) A person has a local connection with the area of a local housing authority in Wales or England if the person has a connection with it—
    (a) because the person is, or in the past was, normally resident there, and that residence is or was of the person's own choice,
    (b) because the person is employed there,
    (c) because of family associations, or
    (d) because of special circumstances.
(3) Residence in an area is not of a person's own choice if the person, or a person who might reasonably be expected to reside with that person, becomes resident there because the person is detained under the authority of an enactment.
(4) The Welsh Ministers may by order specify circumstances in which—
    (a) a person is not to be treated as employed in an area, or
    (b) residence in an area is not to be treated as of a person's own choice.
(5) A person has a local connection with the area of a local housing authority in Wales or England if the person was (at any time) provided with accommodation in that area under section 95 of the Immigration and Asylum Act 1999 (support for asylum seekers).
(6) But subsection (5) does not apply—
    (a) to the provision of accommodation for a person in an area of a local housing authority if the person was subsequently provided with accommodation in the area of another local housing authority under section 95 of that Act, or
    (b) to the provision of accommodation in an accommodation centre by virtue of section 22 of the Nationality, Immigration and Asylum Act 2002 (use of accommodation centres for section 95 support).

Commencement Information

140. S. 81 in force at 1.12.2014 for specified purposes by S.I. 2014/3127, art. 2. (b), Sch. Pt. 2
141. S. 81 in force at 27.4.2015 in so far as not already in force by S.I. 2015/1272, art. 2, Sch. para. 32

82. Duties to applicant whose case is considered for referral or referred

(1) Where a local housing authority notifies an applicant in accordance with section 84 that it intends to notify or has notified another local housing authority in Wales or England of its opinion that the conditions are met for the referral of the applicant's case to that other authority—
    (a) it ceases to be subject to any duty under section 68 (interim duty to secure accommodation

for homeless applicants in priority need), andd
  (b) it is not subject to any duty under section 73 (duty to help to secure accommodation for homeless applicants);
but it must secure that suitable accommodation is available for occupation by the applicant until the applicant is notified of the decision whether the conditions for referral of the case are met.
(2) When it has been decided whether the conditions for referral are met, the notifying authority must notify the applicant in accordance with section 84.
(3) If it is decided that the conditions for referral are not met, the notifying authority is subject to the duty under section 73 (duty to help to secure accommodation for homeless applicants).
(4) If it is decided that those conditions are met and the notified authority is an authority in Wales, the notified authority is subject to the duty under section 73 (duty to help to secure accommodation for homeless applicants); for provision about cases where it is decided that those conditions are met and the notified authority is an authority in England, see section 201. A of the Housing Act 1996 (cases referred from a local housing authority in Wales).
(5) The duty under subsection (1) ceases as provided in that subsection even if the applicant requests a review of the authority's decision (see section 85).
(6) The authority may secure that suitable accommodation is available for the applicant's occupation pending the decision on a review.
(7) If notice required to be given to an applicant under this section is not received by the applicant, it is to be treated as having been given if it is made available at the authority's office for a reasonable period for collection by the applicant or on the applicant's behalf.
Commencement Information
I42. S. 82 in force at 27.4.2015 by S.I. 2015/1272, art. 2, Sch. para. 33
83. Cases referred from a local housing authority in England
(1) This section applies where an application has been referred by a local housing authority in England to a local housing authority in Wales under section 198. (1) of the Housing Act 1996 (referral of case to another local housing authority).
(2) If it is decided that the conditions in that section for referral of the case are met the notified authority is subject to the following duties in respect of the person whose case is referred—
  (a) section 68 (interim duty to secure accommodation for homeless applicants in priority need);
  (b) section 73 (duty to help to secure accommodation for homeless applicants);
for provision about cases where it is decided that the conditions for referral are not met, see section 200 of the Housing Act 1996 (duties to applicant whose case is considered for referral or referred).
(3) Accordingly, references in this Chapter to an applicant include a reference to a person to whom the duties mentioned in subsection (2) are owed by virtue of this section.
Commencement Information
I43. S. 83 in force at 27.4.2015 by S.I. 2015/1272, art. 2, Sch. para. 34

Notice

84. Notice that duties have ended
(1) Where a local housing authority concludes that its duty to an applicant under section 66, 68, 73 or 75 has come to an end (including where the authority has referred the applicant's case to another authority or decided that the conditions for referral are met), it must notify the applicant—
  (a) that it no longer regards itself as being subject to the relevant duty,
  (b) of the reasons why it considers that the duty has come to an end,
  (c) of the right to request a review, and
  (d) of the time within which such a request must be made.
(2) Where a notice under subsection (1) relates to the duty in section 73 coming to an end in the circumstances described in section 74. (2) or (3), it must include notice of the steps taken by the local housing authority to help to secure that suitable accommodation would be available for

occupation by the applicant.
(3) Notice under this section must be in writing.
(4) Where a notice is not received by an applicant, the applicant may be treated as having been notified under this section if the notice is made available at the authority's office for a reasonable period for collection by the applicant or on the applicant's behalf.
Commencement Information
I44. S. 84 in force at 27.4.2015 by S.I. 2015/1272, art. 2, Sch. para. 35

Right to review and appeal

85. Right to request review
(1) An applicant has the right to request a review of the following decisions—
    (a) a decision of a local housing authority as to the applicant's eligibility for help;
    (b) a decision of a local housing authority that a duty is not owed to the applicant under section 66, 68, 73, or 75 (duties to applicants who are homeless or threatened with homelessness);
    (c) a decision of a local housing authority that a duty owed to the applicant under section 66, 68, 73, or 75 has come to an end (including where the authority has referred the applicant's case to another authority or decided that the conditions for referral are met).
(2) Where the duty owed to an applicant under section 73 has come to an end in the circumstances described in section 74. (2) or (3), an applicant has the right to request a review of whether or not reasonable steps were taken during the period in which the duty under section 73 was owed to help to secure that suitable accommodation would be available for his or her occupation.
(3) An applicant who is offered accommodation in, or in connection with, the discharge of any duty under this Chapter may request a review of the suitability of the accommodation offered to the applicant (whether or not he or she has accepted the offer).
(4) There is no right to request a review of the decision reached on an earlier review.
(5) A request for review must be made before the end of the period of 21 days (or such longer period as the authority may in writing allow) beginning with the day on which the applicant is notified of the authority's decision.
(6) On a request being made to them, the authority or authorities concerned must review their decision.
Commencement Information
I45. S. 85 in force at 27.4.2015 by S.I. 2015/1272, art. 2, Sch. para. 36
86. Procedure on review
(1) The Welsh Ministers may make provision by regulations as to the procedure to be followed in connection with a review under section 85.
(2) Regulations under subsection (1) may, for example,—
    (a) require the decision on review to be made by a person of appropriate seniority who was not involved in the original decision, and
    (b) provide for the circumstances in which the applicant is entitled to an oral hearing, and whether and by whom the applicant may be represented at such a hearing, and
    (c) provide for the period within which the review must be carried out and notice given of the decision.
(3) The authority, or as the case may be either of the authorities, concerned must notify the applicant of the decision on the review.
(4) The authority must also notify the applicant of the reasons for the decision, if the decision is—
    (a) to confirm the original decision on any issue against the interests of the applicant, or
    (b) to confirm that reasonable steps were taken.
(5) In any case they must inform the applicant of his or her right to appeal to the county court on a point of law, and of the period within which such an appeal must be made (see section 88).
(6) Notice of the decision is not be treated as given unless and until subsection (5), and where applicable subsection (4), is complied with.

(7) Notice required to be given to a person under this section must be given in writing and, if not received by that person, is to be treated as having been given if it is made available at the authority's office for a reasonable period for collection by the person or on his or her behalf.
Commencement Information
I46. S. 86 in force at 1.12.2014 for specified purposes by S.I. 2014/3127, art. 2. (b), Sch. Pt. 2
I47. S. 86 in force at 27.4.2015 in so far as not already in force by S.I. 2015/1272, art, 2, Sch. para. 37
87. Effect of a decision on review or appeal that reasonable steps were not taken
(1) Subsection (2) applies where it is decided on review under section 85. (2) or on an appeal of a decision under that section that reasonable steps were not taken.
(2) The duty in section 73 applies to the applicant again, with the modification that the 56 day period mentioned in subsection (2) of section 74 is to be interpreted as starting on the day the authority notifies the applicant of its decision on review under section 85. (2) or, on an appeal, on such date as the court may order.
Commencement Information
I48. S. 87 in force at 27.4.2015 by S.I. 2015/1272, art. 2, Sch. para. 38
88. Right of appeal to county court on point of law
(1) An applicant who has requested a review under section 85 may appeal to the county court on any point of law arising from the decision or, as the case may be, the original decision or a question as to whether reasonable steps were taken if the applicant—
 (a) is dissatisfied with the decision on the review, or
 (b) is not notified of the decision on the review within the time prescribed under section 86.
(2) An appeal must be brought within 21 days of the applicant being notified of the decision or, as the case may be, of the date on which the applicant should have been notified of a decision on review.
(3) The court may give permission for an appeal to be brought after the end of the period allowed by subsection (2), but only if it is satisfied—
 (a) where permission is sought before the end of that period, that there is a good reason for the applicant to be unable to bring the appeal in time, or
 (b) where permission is sought after that time, that there is a good reason for the applicant's failure to bring the appeal in time and for any delay in applying for permission.
(4) On appeal the court may make such order confirming, quashing or varying the decision as it thinks fit.
(5) Where the authority was under a duty under section 68, 75 or 82 to secure that suitable accommodation is available for the applicant's occupation, it may secure that suitable accommodation is so available—
 (a) during the period for appealing under this section against the authority's decision, and
 (b) if an appeal is brought, until the appeal (and any further appeal) is finally determined.
Commencement Information
I49. S. 88 in force at 27.4.2015 by S.I. 2015/1272, art. 2, Sch. para. 39
89. Appeals against refusal to accommodate pending appeal
(1) This section applies where an applicant has the right to appeal to the county court under section 88.
(2) An applicant may appeal to the county court against a decision of the authority—
 (a) not to exercise their power under section 88. (5) ("the section 88. (5) power") in the applicant's case,
 (b) to exercise that power for a limited period ending before the final determination by the county court of the applicant's appeal under section 88. (1) ("the main appeal"), or
 (c) to cease exercising that power before the final determination.
(3) An appeal under this section may not be brought after the final determination by the county court of the main appeal.
(4) On an appeal under this section the court—
 (a) may order the authority to secure that suitable accommodation is available for the applicant's

occupation until the determination of the appeal (or such earlier time as the court may specify), and

(b) must confirm or quash the decision appealed against.

(5) In considering whether to confirm or quash the decision the court must apply the principles applied by the High Court on an application for judicial review.

(6) If the court quashes the decision it may order the authority to exercise the section 88. (5) power in the applicant's case for such period as may be specified in the order.

(7) An order under subsection (6)—

(a) may only be made if the court is satisfied that failure to exercise the section 88. (5) power in accordance with the order would substantially prejudice the applicant's ability to pursue the main appeal;

(b) may not specify any period ending after the final determination by the county court of the main appeal.

Commencement Information

I50. S. 89 in force at 27.4.2015 by S.I. 2015/1272, art. 2, Sch. para. 40

Supplementary provisions

90. Charges

A local housing authority may require a person in relation to whom it is discharging its functions under this Chapter—

(a) to pay reasonable charges determined by the authority in respect of accommodation which it secures for the person's occupation (either by making it available itself or otherwise), or

(b) to pay a reasonable amount determined by the authority in respect of sums payable by it for accommodation made available by another person.

Commencement Information

I51. S. 90 in force at 27.4.2015 by S.I. 2015/1272, art. 2, Sch. para. 41

91. Out-of-area placement

(1) A local housing authority must in discharging its functions under this Chapter secure or help to secure that suitable accommodation is available for the occupation of the applicant in its area, so far as is reasonably practicable.

(2) If the authority secures that accommodation is available for the occupation of the applicant outside its area in Wales or England, it must give notice to the local housing authority (whether in Wales or England) in whose area the accommodation is situated.

(3) The notice must state—

(a) the name of the applicant,

(b) the number and description of other persons who normally reside with the applicant as a member of his or her family or might reasonably be expected to reside with the applicant,

(c) the address of the accommodation,

(d) the date on which the accommodation was made available to the applicant, and

(e) which function under this Chapter the authority was discharging in securing that the accommodation is available for the applicant's occupation.

(4) The notice must be in writing, and must be given before the end of the period of 14 days beginning with the day on which the accommodation was made available to the applicant.

Commencement Information

I52. S. 91 in force at 27.4.2015 by S.I. 2015/1272, art. 2, Sch. para. 42

92. Interim accommodation: arrangements with private landlord

(1) This section applies where in carrying out any of its functions under section 68, 82 or 88. (5) (interim accommodation) a local housing authority makes arrangements with a private landlord to provide accommodation.

(2) A tenancy granted to the applicant under the arrangements cannot be an assured tenancy before the end of the period of twelve months beginning with—

(a) the date on which the applicant was notified of the authority's decision under section 63. (1) or 80. (5), or

(b) if there is a review of that decision under section 85 or an appeal to the court under section 88, the date on which the applicant is notified of the decision on review or the appeal is finally determined,

unless, before or during that period, the tenant is notified by the landlord (or in the case of joint landlords, at least one of them) that the tenancy is to be regarded as an assured shorthold tenancy or an assured tenancy other than an assured shorthold tenancy.

Commencement Information

I53. S. 92 in force at 27.4.2015 by S.I. 2015/1272, art. 2, Sch. para. 43

93. Protection of property

(1) Where a local housing authority has become subject to a duty in respect of an applicant as described in subsection (2), it must take reasonable steps to prevent the loss of the personal property of the applicant or prevent or mitigate damage to it if the authority has reason to believe that—

(a) there is danger of loss of, or damage to, the property by reason of the applicant's inability to protect it or deal with it, and

(b) no other suitable arrangements have been or are being made.

(2) The duties in respect of an applicant are—

section 66 (duty to help to prevent an applicant from becoming homeless) in the case of an applicant in priority need;

section 68 (interim duty to secure accommodation for homeless applicants in priority need);

section 75 (duty to secure accommodation for applicants in priority need when the duty in section 73 ends);

section 82 (duties to applicant whose case is considered for referral or referred) in the case of an applicant in priority need.

(3) Where a local housing authority has become subject to the duty in subsection (1), it continues to be subject to that duty even if the duty in respect of the applicant as described in subsection (2) comes to an end.

(4) The duty of a local housing authority under subsection (1) is subject to any conditions it considers appropriate in the particular case, which may include conditions as to—

(a) the making and recovery by the authority of reasonable charges for the action taken, or

(b) the disposal by the authority, in such circumstances as may be specified, of property in relation to which it has taken action.

(5) A local housing authority may take any steps it considers reasonable for the purpose of protecting the personal property of an applicant who is eligible for help or prevent or mitigate damage to it if the authority has reason to believe that—

(a) there is danger of loss of, or damage to, the property by reason of the applicant's inability to protect it or deal with it, and

(b) no other suitable arrangements have been or are being made.

(6) References in this section to personal property of the applicant include personal property of any person who might reasonably be expected to reside with the applicant.

Commencement Information

I54. S. 93 in force at 27.4.2015 by S.I. 2015/1272, art. 2, Sch. para. 44

94. Protection of property: supplementary provisions

(1) The authority may for the purposes of section 93—

(a) enter, at all reasonable times, any premises which are the usual place of residence of the applicant or which were the applicant's last usual place of residence, and

(b) deal with any personal property of the applicant in any way which is reasonably necessary, in particular by storing it or arranging for its storage.

(2) Where a local authority is proposing to exercise the power in subsection (1)(a), the officer it authorises to do so must, upon request, produce valid documentation setting out the authorisation to do so.

(3) A person who, without reasonable excuse, obstructs the exercise of the power under subsection (1)(a) commits an offence and is liable on summary conviction to a fine not exceeding level 4 on the standard scale.

(4) Where the applicant asks the authority to move his or her property to a particular location nominated by the applicant, the authority—

(a) may, if it appears to it that the request is reasonable, discharge its responsibilities under section 93 by doing as the applicant asks, and

(b) having done so, have no further duty or power to take action under that section in relation to that property.

(5) If such a request is made, the authority must before complying with it inform the applicant of the consequence of it doing so.

(6) If no such request is made (or, if made, is not acted upon) the authority cease to have any duty or power to take action under section 93 when, in its opinion, there is no longer any reason to believe that there is a danger of loss of or damage to a person's personal property by reason of his or her inability to protect it or deal with it.

(7) But property stored by virtue of the authority having taken such action may be kept in store and any conditions upon which it was taken into store continue to have effect, with any necessary modifications.

(8) Where the authority—

(a) ceases to be subject to a duty to take action under section 93 in respect of an applicant's property, or

(b) ceases to have power to take such action, having previously taken such action,

it must notify the applicant of that fact and of the reason for it.

(9) The notification must be given to the applicant—

(a) by delivering it to the applicant, or

(b) leaving it at, or sending it to, the applicant's last known address.

(10) References in this section to personal property of the applicant include personal property of any person who might reasonably be expected to reside with the applicant.

Commencement Information

I55. S. 94 in force at 27.4.2015 by S.I. 2015/1272, art. 2, Sch. para. 45

95. Co-operation

(1) A council of a county or county borough in Wales must make arrangements to promote co-operation between the officers of the authority who exercise its social services functions and those who exercise its functions as the local housing authority with a view to achieving the following objectives in its area—

(a) the prevention of homelessness,

(b) that suitable accommodation is or will be available for people who are or may become homeless,

(c) that satisfactory support is available for people who are or may become homeless, and

(d) the effective discharge of its functions under this Part.

(2) If a local housing authority requests the co-operation of a person mentioned in subsection (5) in the exercise of its functions under this Part, the person must comply with the request unless the person considers that doing so would—

(a) be incompatible with the person's own duties, or

(b) otherwise have an adverse effect on the exercise of the person's functions.

(3) If a local housing authority requests that a person mentioned in subsection (5) provides it with information it requires for the purpose of the exercise of any of its functions under this Part, the person must comply with the request unless the person considers that doing so would—

(a) be incompatible with the person's own duties, or

(b) otherwise have an adverse effect on the exercise of the person's functions.

(4) A person who decides not to comply with a request under subsection (2) or (3) must give the local housing authority who made the request written reasons for the decision.

(5) The persons (whether in Wales or England) are—

(a) a local housing authority;
(b) a social services authority;
(c) a registered social landlord;
(d) a new town corporation;
(e) a private registered provider of social housing;
(f) a housing action trust.

(6) The Welsh Ministers may amend subsection (5) by order to omit or add a person, or a description of a person.

(7) An order under subsection (6) may not add a Minister of the Crown.

(8) In this section—

"housing action trust" ("ymddiriedolaeth gweithredu tai") means a housing action trust established under Part 3 of the Housing Act 1988;

"new town corporation" ("corfforaeth tref newydd") has the meaning given in Part 1 of the Housing Act 1985;

"private registered provider of social housing" ("darparwr tai cymdeithasol preifat cofrestredig") has the meaning given by Part 2 of the Housing and Regeneration Act 2008;

"registered social landlord" ("landlord cymdeithasol cofrestredig") has the meaning given by Part 1 of the Housing Act 1996.

Commencement Information

I56. S. 95 in force at 1.12.2014 for specified purposes by S.I. 2014/3127, art. 2. (b), Sch. Pt. 2
I57. S. 95 in force at 27.4.2015 in so far as not already in force by S.I. 2015/1272, art. 2, Sch. para. 46

96. Co-operation in certain cases involving children

(1) This section applies where a local housing authority has reason to believe that an applicant with whom a person under the age of 18 normally resides, or might reasonably be expected to reside—

(a) may be ineligible for help,
(b) may be homeless and that a duty under section 68, 73 or 75 is not likely to apply to the applicant, or
(c) may be threatened with homelessness and that a duty under section 66 is not likely to apply to the applicant.

(2) A local housing authority must make arrangements for ensuring that—

(a) the applicant is invited to consent to the referral to the social services department of the essential facts of his or her case, and
(b) if the applicant has given that consent, the social services department is made aware of those facts and of the subsequent decision of the authority in respect of his or her case.

(3) Nothing in subsection (2) affects any power apart from this section to disclose information relating to the applicant's case to the the social services department without the consent of the applicant.

(4) A council of a county or county borough must make arrangements for ensuring that, where it makes a decision as local housing authority that an applicant is ineligible for help, became homeless intentionally or became threatened with homelessness intentionally, its housing department provides the social services department with such advice and assistance as the social services department may reasonably request.

(5) In this section, in relation to the council of a county or county borough—

"the housing department" ("yr adran dai") means those persons responsible for the exercise of its functions as local housing authority;

"the social services department" ("yr adran gwasanaethau cymdeithasol") means those persons responsible for the exercise of its social services functions under Part 3 of the Social Services and Well-Being (Wales) Act 2014.

Commencement Information

I58. S. 96 in force at 27.4.2015 by S.I. 2015/1272, art. 2, Sch. para. 47

General

97. False statements, withholding information and failure to disclose change of circumstances

(1) It is an offence for a person, with intent to induce a local housing authority to believe in connection with the exercise of its functions under this Chapter that the person or another person is entitled to accommodation or assistance in accordance with the provisions of this Chapter, or is entitled to accommodation or assistance of a particular description—

(a) knowingly or recklessly to make a statement which is false in a material particular, or

(b) knowingly to withhold information which the authority has reasonably required the person to give in connection with the exercise of those functions.

(2) If before an applicant receives notification of the local housing authority's decision on the application there is any change of facts material to the case, the applicant must notify the authority as soon as possible.

(3) The authority must explain to every applicant, in ordinary language, the duty imposed by subsection (2) and the effect of subsection (4).

(4) A person who fails to comply with subsection (2) after being given the explanation required by subsection (3) commits an offence.

(5) In proceedings against a person for an offence committed under subsection (4) it is a defence that the person had a reasonable excuse for failing to comply.

(6) A person guilty of an offence under this section is liable on summary conviction to a fine not exceeding level 4 on the standard scale.

Commencement Information

I59. S. 97 in force at 27.4.2015 by S.I. 2015/1272, art. 2, Sch. para. 48

98. Guidance

(1) In the exercise of its functions relating to homelessness, a council of a county or county borough must have regard to guidance given by the Welsh Ministers.

(2) Subsection (1) applies in relation to functions under this Part and any other enactment.

(3) The Welsh Ministers may—

(a) give guidance either generally or to specified descriptions of authorities;

(b) revise the guidance by giving further guidance under this Part;

(c) withdraw the guidance by giving further guidance under this Part or by notice.

(4) The Welsh Ministers must publish any guidance or notice under this Part.

Commencement Information

I60. S. 98 in force at 1.12.2014 for specified purposes by S.I. 2014/3127, art. 2. (c), Sch. Pt. 3

I61. S. 98 in force at 27.4.2015 in so far as not already in force by S.I. 2015/1272, art. 2, Sch. para. 49

99. Interpretation of this Chapter and index of defined terms

In this Chapter—

"abuse" ("camdriniaeth") has the meaning given by section 58;

"accommodation available for occupation" ("llety sydd ar gael i'w feddiannu") has the meaning given by section 56;

"applicant" ("ceisydd") has the meaning given by section 62. (3) and section 83. (3);

"associated" ("cysylltiedig"), in relation to a person, has the meaning given by section 58;

"assured tenancy" ("tenantiaeth sicr") and "assured shorthold tenancy" ("tenantiaeth fyrddaliol sicr") have the meaning given by Part 1 of the Housing Act 1988;

"domestic abuse" ("camdriniaeth ddomestig") has the meaning given by section 58;

"eligible for help" ("yn gymwys i gael cymorth") means not excluded from help under this Chapter by Schedule 2;

"enactment" ("deddfiad") means an enactment (whenever enacted or made) comprised in, or in an instrument made under—

- an Act of Parliament,
- a Measure or an Act of the National Assembly for Wales;

"help to secure" ("cynorthwyo i sicrhau"), in relation to securing that suitable accommodation is available, or does not cease to be available, for occupation, has the meaning given by section 65;
"help under this Chapter" ("cynorth o dan y Bennod hon") means the benefit of any function under sections 66, 68, 73, or 75;
"homeless" ("digartref") has the meaning given by section 55 and "homelessness" (digartrefedd) is to be interpreted accordingly;
"intentionally homeless" ("digartref yn fwriadol") has the meaning given by section 77;
"local connection" ("cysylltiad lleol") has the meaning given by section 81;
"local housing authority" ("awdurdod tai lleol") means—
   - in relation to Wales, the council of a county or county borough, and
   - in relation to England, a district council, a London borough council, the Common Council of the City of London or the Council of the Isles of Scilly,
but a reference to a "local housing authority" is to be interpreted as a reference to a local housing authority for an area in Wales only, unless this Chapter expressly provides otherwise;
"looked after, accommodated or fostered" ("yn derbyn gofal, yn cael ei letya neu'n cael ei faethu") has the meaning given by section 70. (2);
"prescribed" ("rhagnodedig") means prescribed in regulations made by the Welsh Ministers;
"priority need for accommodation" ("angen blaenoriaethol am lety") has the meaning given by section 70;
"prison" ("carchar") has the same meaning as in the Prison Act 1952 (see section 53. (1) of that Act);
"private landlord" ("landlord preifat") means a landlord who is not within section 80. (1) of the Housing Act 1985 (the landlord condition for secure tenancies);
"reasonable to continue to occupy accommodation" ("rhesymol parhau i feddiannu llety") has the meaning given by section 57;
"regular armed forces of the Crown" ("lluoedd arfog rheolaidd y Goron") means the regular forces as defined by section 374 of the Armed Forces Act 2006;
"restricted person" ("person cyfyngedig") has the meaning given by section 63. (5);
"social services authority" ("awdurdod gwasanaethau cymdeithasol") means—
   - in relation to Wales, the council of a county or county borough council in the exercise of its social services functions, within the meaning of section 119 of the Social Services and Well-being (Wales) Act 2014, and
   - in relation to England, a local authority for the purposes of the Local Authority Social Services Act 1970, as defined in section 1 of that Act,
but a reference to a "social services authority" is to be interpreted as a reference to a social services authority for an area in Wales only, unless this Chapter expressly provides otherwise;
"threatened with homelessness" ("o dan fygythiad o ddigartrefedd") has the meaning given by section 55. (4);
"voluntary organisation" ("corff gwirfoddol") means a body (other than a public or local authority) whose activities are not carried on for profit.
"youth detention accommodation" ("llety cadw ieuenctid") means—
   - a secure children's home;
   - a secure training centre;
   - a young offender institution;
   - accommodation provided, equipped and maintained by the Welsh Ministers under section 82. (5) of the Children Act 1989 for the purpose of restricting the liberty of children;
   - accommodation, or accommodation of a description, for the time being specified by order under section 107. (1)(e) of the Powers of Criminal Courts (Sentencing) Act 2000 (youth detention accommodation for the purposes of detention and training orders).
Commencement Information
162. S. 99 in force at 1.12.2014 for specified purposes by S.I. 2014/3127, art. 2. (b), Sch. Pt. 2
163. S. 99 in force at 27.4.2015 in so far as not already in force by S.I. 2015/1272, art. 2, Sch. para. 50

100. Consequential amendments
Part 1 of Schedule 3 makes consequential amendments relating to this Part.
Commencement Information
I64. S. 100 in force at 27.4.2015 by S.I. 2015/1272, art. 2, Sch. para. 51

PART 3. GYPSIES AND TRAVELLERS

PART 3 GYPSIES AND TRAVELLERS

101. Assessment of accommodation needs

(1) A local housing authority must, in each review period, carry out an assessment of the accommodation needs of Gypsies and Travellers residing in or resorting to its area.
(2) In carrying out an assessment under subsection (1) a local housing authority must consult such persons as it considers appropriate.
(3) In subsection (1), "review period" means—
 (a) the period of 1 year beginning with the coming into force of this section, and
 (b) each subsequent period of 5 years.
(4) The Welsh Ministers may amend subsection (3)(b) by order.
Commencement Information
I1. S. 101 in force at 25.2.2015 by S.I. 2015/380, art. 2. (a)

102. Report following assessment

(1) After carrying out an assessment a local housing authority must prepare a report which—
 (a) details how the assessment was carried out;
 (b) contains a summary of—
(i) the consultation it carried out in connection with the assessment, and
(ii) the responses (if any) it received to that consultation;
 (c) details the accommodation needs identified by the assessment.
(2) A local housing authority must submit the report to the Welsh Ministers for approval of the authority's assessment.
(3) The Welsh Ministers may—
 (a) approve the assessment as submitted;
 (b) approve the assessment with modifications;
 (c) reject the assessment.
(4) If the Welsh Ministers reject the assessment, the local housing authority must—
 (a) revise and resubmit its assessment for approval by the Welsh Ministers under subsection (3), or
 (b) conduct another assessment (in which case section 101. (2) and this section apply again, as if the assessment were carried out under section 101. (1)).
(5) A local housing authority must publish an assessment approved by the Welsh Ministers under this section.
Commencement Information
I2. S. 102 in force at 25.2.2015 by S.I. 2015/380, art. 2. (b)

103. Duty to meet assessed needs

(1) If a local housing authority's approved assessment identifies needs within the authority's area with respect to the provision of sites on which mobile homes may be stationed the authority must exercise its powers in section 56 of the Mobile Homes (Wales) Act 2013 (power of authorities to provide sites for mobile homes) so far as may be necessary to meet those needs.
(2) But subsection (1) does not require a local housing authority to provide, in or in connection with sites for the stationing of mobile homes, working space and facilities for the carrying on of activities normally carried out by Gypsies and Travellers.
(3) The reference in subsection (1) to an authority's approved assessment is a reference to the authority's most recent assessment of accommodation needs approved by the Welsh Ministers under section 102. (3).
Commencement Information
I3. S. 103 in force at 16.3.2016 by S.I. 2016/266, art. 2. (a)

104. Failure to comply with duty under section 103.

(1) If the Welsh Ministers are satisfied that a local housing authority has failed to comply with the duty imposed by section 103 they may direct the authority to exercise its powers under section 56 of the Mobile Homes (Wales) Act 2013 so far as may be necessary to meet the needs identified in the authority's approved assessment.
(2) Before giving a direction the Welsh Ministers must consult the local housing authority to which the direction would relate.
(3) A local housing authority must comply with a direction given to it.
(4) A direction given under this section—
   (a) must be in writing;
   (b) may be varied or revoked by a subsequent direction;
   (c) is enforceable by mandatory order on application by, or on behalf of, the Welsh Ministers.
Commencement Information
I4. S. 104 in force at 16.3.2016 by S.I. 2016/266, art. 2. (b)

105. Provision of information upon request

(1) A local housing authority must provide the Welsh Ministers with such information (and at such times) as they may require in connection with the exercise of their functions under this Part.
(2) The Welsh Ministers may exercise their powers under this section generally or in relation to a particular case.
Commencement Information
I5. S. 105 in force at 25.2.2015 by S.I. 2015/380, art. 2. (c)

106. Guidance

(1) In exercising its functions under this Part, a local housing authority must have regard to any guidance given by the Welsh Ministers.
(2) The Welsh Ministers may—
   (a) give guidance either generally or to specified descriptions of authorities;
   (b) revise the guidance by giving further guidance under this section;
   (c) withdraw the guidance by giving further guidance under this section or by notice.
(3) The Welsh Ministers must publish any guidance or notice under this section.
Commencement Information
I6. S. 106 in force at 1.12.2014 for specified purposes by S.I. 2014/3127, art. 2. (c), Sch. Pt. 3
I7. S. 106 in force at 25.2.2015 in so far as not already in force by S.I. 2015/380, art. 2. (d)

107. Duties in relation to housing strategies

(1) This section applies where a local housing authority is required under section 87 of the Local Government Act 2003 to have a strategy in respect of meeting the accommodation needs of Gypsies and Travellers residing in or resorting to its area.
(2) The local housing authority must—
    (a) have regard to any guidance given by the Welsh Ministers in preparing its strategy;
    (b) take the strategy into account in exercising its functions (including functions exercisable other than as a local housing authority).
Commencement Information
I8. S. 107 in force at 25.2.2015 by S.I. 2015/380, art. 2. (e)

General

108. Interpretation

In this Part—
"accommodation needs" ("anghenion llety") includes, but is not limited to, needs with respect to the provision of sites on which mobile homes may be stationed;
"Gypsies and Travellers" ("Sipsiwn a Theithwyr") means—
    - persons of a nomadic habit of life, whatever their race or origin, including—
persons who, on grounds only of their own or their family's or dependant's educational or health needs or old age, have ceased to travel temporarily or permanently, and
members of an organised group of travelling show people or circus people (whether or not travelling together as such), and
    - all other persons with a cultural tradition of nomadism or of living in a mobile home;
"mobile home" ("cartref symudol") has the meaning given by section 60 of the Mobile Homes (Wales) Act 2013.
Commencement Information
I9. S. 108 in force at 25.2.2015 by S.I. 2015/380, art. 2. (f)

109. Power to amend definition of Gypsies and Travellers

(1) The Welsh Ministers may by order amend the definition of Gypsies and Travellers in section 108 by—
    (a) adding a description of persons;
    (b) modifying a description of persons;
    (c) removing a description of persons.
(2) An order under this section may also make such amendments of the Mobile Homes (Wales) Act 2013 as the Welsh Ministers consider necessary or appropriate in consequence of a change to the definition mentioned in subsection (1).
Commencement Information
I10. S. 109 in force at 25.2.2015 by S.I. 2015/380, art. 2. (g)

110. Consequential amendments

Part 2 of Schedule 3 makes consequential amendments relating to this Part.
Commencement Information
I11. S. 110 in force at 25.2.2015 by S.I. 2015/380, art. 2. (h)

PART 4. STANDARDS FOR SOCIAL HOUSING

PART 4 STANDARDS FOR SOCIAL HOUSING

111. Standards

(1) The Welsh Ministers may set standards to be met by local housing authorities in connection with—
   (a) the quality of accommodation provided by local housing authorities for housing;
   (b) rent for such accommodation;
   (c) service charges for such accommodation.
(2) Standards set under subsection (1) may require local housing authorities to comply with rules specified in the standards.
(3) Rules about rent or service charges may include, among other things, provision for minimum or maximum—
   (a) levels of rent or service charges,
   (b) levels of increase or decrease of rent or service charges.
(4) The Welsh Ministers may—
   (a) revise the standards by issuing further standards under this section;
   (b) withdraw the standards by issuing further standards under this section or by notice.
(5) The Welsh Ministers must publish standards or notices under this section.
Commencement Information
I1. S. 111 in force at 1.12.2014 by S.I. 2014/3127, art. 2. (a), Sch. Pt. 1

112. Guidance

(1) The Welsh Ministers may give guidance that—
   (a) relates to a matter addressed by a standard under section 111, and
   (b) amplifies the standard.
(2) In considering whether standards have been met the Welsh Ministers may have regard to the guidance.
(3) The Welsh Ministers may—
   (a) revise the guidance by giving further guidance under this section;
   (b) withdraw the guidance by giving further guidance under this section or by notice.
(4) The Welsh Ministers must publish any guidance or notice under this section.
Commencement Information
I2. S. 112 in force at 1.12.2014 by S.I. 2014/3127, art. 2. (a), Sch. Pt. 1

113. Consultation on standards and guidance

Before setting, revising or withdrawing standards under section 111 or issuing, revising or withdrawing guidance under section 112, the Welsh Ministers must consult—
   (a) one or more bodies appearing to them to represent the interests of local housing authorities,
   (b) one or more bodies appearing to them to represent the interests of tenants, and
   (c) any other persons the Welsh Ministers consider it appropriate to consult.
Commencement Information
I3. S. 113 in force at 1.12.2014 by S.I. 2014/3127, art. 2. (a), Sch. Pt. 1

114. Information on compliance with standards

A local housing authority must provide the Welsh Ministers with any information they request relating to compliance by the authority with standards set under section 111.
Commencement Information
I4. S. 114 in force at 1.12.2014 by S.I. 2014/3127, art. 2. (a), Sch. Pt. 1

115. Powers of entry

(1) This section applies where it appears to the Welsh Ministers that a local housing authority may be failing to maintain or repair any premises in accordance with standards set under section 111 or guidance given under section 112.
(2) A person authorised by the Welsh Ministers may at any reasonable time, on giving not less than 28 days' notice of his or her intention to the local housing authority concerned, enter any such premises for the purpose of survey and examination.
(3) Where such notice is given to the local housing authority, the authority must give the occupier or occupiers of the premises not less than seven days' notice of the proposed survey and examination.
(4) An authorisation for the purposes of this section must be in writing stating the particular purpose or purposes for which the entry is authorised and must, if so required, be produced for inspection by the occupier or anyone acting on his or her behalf.
(5) The Welsh Ministers must give a copy of any survey carried out in exercise of the powers conferred by this section to the local housing authority concerned.
(6) The Welsh Ministers may require the local housing authority concerned to pay to them such amount as the Welsh Ministers may determine towards the costs of carrying out any survey under this section.
Commencement Information
I5. S. 115 in force at 1.12.2014 by S.I. 2014/3127, art. 2. (a), Sch. Pt. 1

116. Exercise of intervention powers

(1) This section applies where the Welsh Ministers are deciding—
    (a) whether to exercise an intervention power,
    (b) which intervention power to exercise, or
    (c) how to exercise an intervention power.
(2) The Welsh Ministers must consider—
    (a) whether the failure or likely failure to meet the standard is, or is likely to be, a recurrent or isolated incident;
    (b) the speed with which the failure, or likely failure to meet the standard needs to be addressed.
(3) In subsection (1), an "intervention power" means a power exercisable under sections 117 to 127.
Commencement Information
I6. S. 116 in force at 1.12.2014 by S.I. 2014/3127, art. 2. (a), Sch. Pt. 1

117. Grounds for intervention

For the purposes of this Part, the grounds for intervention are that a local housing authority has failed, or is likely to fail, to meet a standard set under section 111 which relates to the quality of accommodation.
Commencement Information
I7. S. 117 in force at 1.12.2014 by S.I. 2014/3127, art. 2. (a), Sch. Pt. 1

118. Warning notice

(1) The Welsh Ministers may give a warning notice to a local housing authority if they are satisfied that the grounds for intervention exist in relation to the authority.
(2) The Welsh Ministers must specify each of the following in the warning notice—
    (a) the reasons why they are satisfied that the grounds exist;
    (b) the action they require the authority to take in order to deal with the grounds for intervention;
    (c) the period within which the action is to be taken by the authority ("the compliance period");
    (d) the action they are minded to take if the authority fails to take the required action.
Commencement Information
I8. S. 118 in force at 1.12.2014 by S.I. 2014/3127, art. 2. (a), Sch. Pt. 1

119. Power of Welsh Ministers to intervene

(1) The Welsh Ministers have the power to intervene under this Part if—
    (a) the Welsh Ministers have given a warning notice, and
    (b) the local housing authority has failed to comply, or secure compliance, with the notice to the Welsh Ministers' satisfaction within the compliance period.
(2) Where the Welsh Ministers have the power to intervene, they must keep the circumstances giving rise to the power under review.
(3) If the Welsh Ministers conclude that the grounds for intervention have been dealt with to their satisfaction or that exercise of their powers under this Part would not be appropriate for any other reason, they must notify the local housing authority of their conclusion in writing.
(4) The Welsh Ministers' power to intervene continues in effect until they give notice under subsection (3).
(5) Where the Welsh Ministers have the power to intervene, they are not limited to taking the action they said they were minded to take in a warning notice.
Commencement Information
I9. S. 119 in force at 1.12.2014 by S.I. 2014/3127, art. 2. (a), Sch. Pt. 1

120. Power to require local housing authority to obtain advisory services

(1) This section applies if the Welsh Ministers have the power to intervene.
(2) The Welsh Ministers may direct the local housing authority to enter into a contract or other arrangement with a specified person, or a person falling within a specified class, for the provision to the authority, of specified services of an advisory nature.
(3) The direction may require the contract or other arrangement to contain specified terms and conditions.
(4) In this section and section 121 "specified" means specified in a direction.
Commencement Information
I10. S. 120 in force at 1.12.2014 by S.I. 2014/3127, art. 2. (a), Sch. Pt. 1

121. Power to require performance of functions by other persons on behalf of authority

(1) This section applies if the Welsh Ministers have the power to intervene.
(2) The Welsh Ministers may give such directions to the local housing authority or any of its

officers as they think are appropriate for securing that the functions to which the grounds for intervention relate are performed on behalf of the authority by a person specified in the direction.
(3) A direction under subsection (2) may require that any contract or other arrangement made by the authority with the specified person contains terms and conditions specified in the direction.
Commencement Information
I11. S. 121 in force at 1.12.2014 by S.I. 2014/3127, art. 2. (a), Sch. Pt. 1

122. Power to require performance of functions by Welsh Ministers or nominee

(1) This section applies if the Welsh Ministers have the power to intervene.
(2) The Welsh Ministers may direct that the functions to which the grounds for intervention relate are to be exercised by the Welsh Ministers or a person nominated by them.
(3) If a direction is made under subsection (2), the local housing authority must comply with the instructions of the Welsh Ministers or their nominee in relation to the exercise of the functions.
Commencement Information
I12. S. 122 in force at 1.12.2014 by S.I. 2014/3127, art. 2. (a), Sch. Pt. 1

123. Power to direct exercise of other local housing authority functions

(1) If the Welsh Ministers think it is expedient, a direction under section 121 or 122 may relate to the performance of functions of the local housing authority in addition to the functions to which the grounds for intervention relate.
(2) The Welsh Ministers may have regard (among other things) to financial considerations in deciding whether it is expedient that a direction should relate to the functions of the local housing authority other than functions relating to the grounds for intervention.
Commencement Information
I13. S. 123 in force at 1.12.2014 by S.I. 2014/3127, art. 2. (a), Sch. Pt. 1

124. General power to give directions and take steps

(1) This section applies if the Welsh Ministers have the power to intervene.
(2) If the Welsh Ministers think it is appropriate in order to deal with the grounds for intervention, the Welsh Ministers may—
    (a) give directions to the local housing authority or any of its officers, or
    (b) take any other steps.
Commencement Information
I14. S. 124 in force at 1.12.2014 by S.I. 2014/3127, art. 2. (a), Sch. Pt. 1

125. Directions

(1) A local housing authority, or an officer of an authority, subject to a direction or instruction under this Part must comply with it.
(2) This includes a direction or an instruction to exercise a power or duty that is contingent upon the opinion of the authority or an officer of the authority.
(3) A direction under this Part—
    (a) must be in writing;
    (b) may be varied or revoked by a later direction;
    (c) is enforceable by mandatory order on application by, or on behalf of, the Welsh Ministers.

Commencement Information

I15. S. 125 in force at 1.12.2014 by S.I. 2014/3127, art. 2. (a), Sch. Pt. 1

126. Duty to co-operate

(1) A local housing authority must give the Welsh Ministers and any person mentioned in subsection (2) as much assistance in connection with the exercise of functions under or by virtue of this Part as they are reasonably able to give.
(2) The persons are—
 (a) any person authorised for the purposes of this section by the Welsh Ministers;
 (b) any person acting under directions under this Part;
 (c) any person assisting—
(i) the Welsh Ministers, or
(ii) a person mentioned in paragraph (a) or (b).
Commencement Information
I16. S. 126 in force at 1.12.2014 by S.I. 2014/3127, art. 2. (a), Sch. Pt. 1

127. Powers of entry and inspection

(1) A person falling within subsection (2) has at all reasonable times—
 (a) a right of entry to the premises of the local housing authority (other than a dwelling) in question;
 (b) a right to inspect, and take copies of, any records or other documents kept by the authority, and any other documents containing information relating to the authority, which the person considers relevant to the exercise of his or her functions under or by virtue of this Part.
(2) The following persons fall within this subsection—
 (a) a person specified in a direction under section 120 or, where the direction specifies a class of persons, the person with whom the local housing authority enter into the contract or other arrangement required by the direction;
 (b) a person specified in a direction under section 121;
 (c) the Welsh Ministers in pursuance of a direction under section 122;
 (d) a person nominated by direction under section 122.
(3) In exercising the right under subsection (1)(b) to inspect records or other documents, a person ("P")—
 (a) is entitled to have access to, and inspect and check the operation of, any computer and any associated apparatus or material which is or has been in use in connection with the records or other documents in question, and
 (b) may require the following persons to provide any assistance P may reasonably require (including, among other things, the making of information available for inspection or copying in a legible form)—
(i) the person by whom or on whose behalf the computer is or has been so used;
(ii) any person having charge of, or otherwise concerned with the operation of, the computer, apparatus or material.
(4) Any reference in this section to a person falling within subsection (2) includes a reference to any person assisting that person.
(5) In this section "document" and "records" each include information recorded in any form.
Commencement Information
I17. S. 127 in force at 1.12.2014 by S.I. 2014/3127, art. 2. (a), Sch. Pt. 1

Service charges for social housing

128. Exemption from offences relating to service charges for social housing

In section 25 of the Landlord and Tenant Act 1985, after subsection (2) insert—
"(3)Subsection (1) does not apply where the person is—
   (a) a local authority for an area in Wales, or
   (b) a registered social landlord."
Commencement Information
I18. S. 128 in force at 1.12.2014 by S.I. 2014/3127, art. 2. (a), Sch. Pt. 1
Prospective

129. Application of duties relating to service charges to local authority tenancies

In section 26. (1) of the Landlord and Tenant Act 1985, after "a local authority" insert " for an area in England ".

General

130. Consequential amendments

Part 3 of Schedule 3 makes consequential amendments relating to this Part.
Commencement Information
I19. S. 130 in force at 1.12.2014 by S.I. 2014/3127, art. 2. (a), Sch. Pt. 1

PART 5. HOUSING FINANCE

PART 5 HOUSING FINANCE

131. Abolition of Housing Revenue Account subsidy

(1) This section provides for the abolition of the subsidy payable in relation to the Housing Revenue Accounts of local housing authorities under the Local Government and Housing Act 1989.
(2) That Act is amended as follows.
(3) In Part 6 (Housing Finance)—
   (a) omit section 79 (Housing Revenue Account subsidy);
   (b) omit section 80 (calculation of Housing Revenue Account subsidy);
   (c) omit section 80. ZA (negative amounts of subsidy payable to appropriate person);
   (d) omit section 80. A (final decision on amount of Housing Revenue Account subsidy);
   (e) omit section 80. B (agreements to exclude certain authorities or property);
   (f) omit section 85 (power to obtain information);
   (g) omit section 86 (recoupment of subsidy in certain cases).
(4) In Schedule 4 (the keeping of the Housing Revenue Account)—
   (a) in Part 1 (credits to the Account), omit Item 3 (Housing Revenue Account subsidy);

(b) in Part 2 (debits to the Account), omit Item 5 (sums payable under section 80. ZA);
(c) in Part 3 (special cases), omit paragraph 2 (credit balance where no HRA subsidy payable) and the heading immediately before it.
Commencement Information
I1. S. 131. (4)(c) in force at 1.12.2014 by S.I. 2014/3127, art. 2. (a), Sch. Pt. 1

Payments in relation to Housing Revenue Accounts

132. Settlement payments

(1) The Welsh Ministers may make a determination providing for the calculation of the amount of a payment in relation to each local housing authority that keeps a Housing Revenue Account.
(2) A payment of the type mentioned in subsection (1) is referred to in this Part as a "settlement payment".
(3) A determination under this section may provide for all or part of the amount to be calculated in accordance with a formula or formulae.
(4) In determining a formula for this purpose, the Welsh Ministers may include variables framed by reference to such matters as they consider appropriate.
(5) A determination under this section may provide that the effect of the calculation in relation to a local housing authority is that—
    (a) a settlement payment must be made by the Welsh Ministers to the local housing authority,
    (b) a settlement payment must be made by the local housing authority to the Welsh Ministers, or
    (c) the amount of a settlement payment in relation to that authority is nil.
(6) Subsections (3), (4) and (5) do not limit the generality of the power conferred by subsection (1).

133. Further payments

(1) If a settlement payment has been made in respect of a local housing authority, the Welsh Ministers may from time to time make a determination that a further payment calculated in accordance with the determination must be made—
    (a) by the Welsh Ministers to the local housing authority, or
    (b) by the local housing authority to the Welsh Ministers.
(2) But the Welsh Ministers may only make a determination under this section if subsection (3) or (4) applies.
(3) This subsection applies if there has been a change in any matter that was taken into account in making—
    (a) the determination relating to the settlement payment or a calculation under that determination, or
    (b) a previous determination under this section relating to the local housing authority or a calculation under that determination.
(4) This subsection applies if the Welsh Ministers are satisfied that an error was taken into account in making any determination or calculation mentioned in subsection (3).
(5) A determination under this section may be varied or revoked by a subsequent determination.

134. Additional provision about payments

(1) A payment under this Part must be made in such instalments, at such times and in accordance with such arrangements as the Welsh Ministers may determine.
(2) A payment under this Part by a local housing authority must be accompanied by such

information as the Welsh Ministers may require.
(3) The Welsh Ministers may charge a local housing authority interest, at such rates and for such periods as the Welsh Ministers may determine, on any sum payable by the local housing authority under this Part not being paid by a time determined under this section for its payment.
(4) The Welsh Ministers may charge a local housing authority an amount equal to any additional costs incurred by the Welsh Ministers as a result of any sum payable by the local housing authority under this Part not being paid by a time determined under this section for its payment.
(5) A payment under this Part other than a payment under subsection (3) or (4)—
    (a) if made by a local housing authority, is to be treated by the authority as capital expenditure for the purposes of Chapter 1 of Part 1 of the Local Government Act 2003;
    (b) if made to a local housing authority, is to be treated by the authority as a capital receipt for the purposes of that Chapter.
(6) A determination under this Part may require a payment to a local housing authority made under this Part to be used by the authority for a purpose specified in the determination.
(7) A local housing authority to which such a requirement applies must comply with it.
(8) In Schedule 4 to the Local Government and Housing Act 1989 (the keeping of the Housing Revenue Account), in Part 2 (debits to the account) after Item 5. A (sums payable under section 170 of the Localism Act 2011) insert— " Item 5. B: sums payable under section 134 of the Housing (Wales) Act 2014 Sums payable for the year to the Welsh Ministers under section 134. (3) or (4) of the Housing (Wales) Act 2014 (interest etc charged as a result of late payment of settlement payments etc). "

General provision

135. Provision of information upon request

(1) A local housing authority must supply the Welsh Ministers with such information as the Welsh Ministers may specify for the purpose of enabling the Welsh Ministers to exercise functions under this Part.
(2) The Welsh Ministers may exercise their powers under this section generally or in relation to a particular case.
(3) If a local housing authority fails to comply with this section before the end of such period as the Welsh Ministers may specify, the Welsh Ministers may exercise functions under this Part on the basis of such assumptions and estimates as the Welsh Ministers think fit.

136. Determinations under this Part

(1) A determination under this Part may make different provision for different cases or descriptions of case, including different provision—
    (a) for different areas;
    (b) for different local housing authorities;
    (c) for different descriptions of local housing authority.
(2) Before making a determination under this Part that relates to all local housing authorities or a description of local housing authority, the Welsh Ministers must consult such—
    (a) representatives of local government in Wales, and
    (b) other persons,
as the Welsh Ministers consider appropriate.
(3) Before making a determination under this Part relating to a particular local housing authority, the Welsh Ministers must consult that local housing authority.
(4) As soon as is practicable after making a determination under this Part, the Welsh Ministers

must send a copy of the determination to the local housing authority or authorities to which it relates.
(5) Subsections (4) to (7) of section 87 of the Local Government and Housing Act 1989 (using electronic communications to send copies of determinations) apply to a determination under this Part as they apply to a determination made by the Welsh Ministers under Part 6 of that Act.

PART 6. ALLOWING FULLY MUTUAL HOUSING ASSOCIATIONS TO GRANT ASSURED TENANCIES

PART 6 ALLOWING FULLY MUTUAL HOUSING ASSOCIATIONS TO GRANT ASSURED TENANCIES

137. Amendment of Schedule 1 to the Housing Act 1988.

(1) Schedule 1 to the Housing Act 1988 (tenancies which cannot be assured tenancies) is amended as follows.
(2) In paragraph 12. (1)(h), after "association" insert " , unless the tenancy is one which is excluded from this sub-paragraph by sub-paragraph (3) below ".
(3) After paragraph 12. (2) insert—
"(3) A tenancy is excluded from sub-paragraph (1) if all of the following requirements are met—
   (a) the interest of the landlord belongs to a fully mutual housing association;
   (b) the dwelling-house is in Wales;
   (c) the tenancy is granted on or after the date on which this sub-paragraph comes into force;
   (d) the tenancy is in writing;
   (e) before the tenancy is granted, the landlord has served on the person who is to be the tenant a notice stating that the tenancy is to be excluded from sub-paragraph (1);
   (f) the tenancy states that it is excluded from sub-paragraph (1)."
Commencement Information
I1. S. 137 in force at 1.12.2014 by S.I. 2014/3127, art. 2. (a), Sch. Pt. 1
Prospective

138. Amendment of Schedule 2 to the Housing Act 1988.

In Part 1 of Schedule 2 to the Housing Act 1988 (grounds on which a court must order possession of dwelling-houses let on assured tenancies), after Ground 2 insert—
The dwelling-house is subject to a mortgage granted, at any time, by a fully mutual housing association and—
(a) the dwelling-house is in Wales;
(b) the tenancy was granted by a fully mutual housing association;
(c) the mortgagee is entitled to exercise a power of sale conferred on the mortgagee by the mortgage or by section 101 of the Law of Property Act 1925;
(d) the mortgagee requires possession of the dwelling-house for the purpose of disposing of it with vacant possession in exercise of that power;
(e) not later than the beginning of the tenancy the landlord gave notice in writing to the tenant that possession might be recovered on this ground;
and for the purposes of this ground "mortgage" includes a charge and "mortgagee" is to be

construed accordingly."

PART 7. COUNCIL TAX FOR CERTAIN TYPES OF DWELLING

PART 7 COUNCIL TAX FOR CERTAIN TYPES OF DWELLING

139. Amount of tax payable for certain types of dwelling

(1) The Local Government Finance Act 1992 is amended as follows.
(2) After section 12 (discounts: special provision for Wales), insert—

"12. AHigher amount for long-term empty dwellings: Wales

(1) For any financial year, a billing authority in Wales may by determination provide in relation to its area that if on any day a dwelling is a long-term empty dwelling—
   (a) the discount under section 11. (2)(a) does not apply, and
   (b) the amount of council tax payable in respect of that dwelling and that day is increased by such percentage of not more than 100 as it may specify in the determination.
(2) A billing authority may specify different percentages for different dwellings based on the length of time for which they have been long-term empty dwellings.
(3) In exercising its functions under this section a billing authority must have regard to any guidance issued by the Welsh Ministers.
(4) The Welsh Ministers may, by regulations, prescribe one or more classes of dwelling in relation to which a billing authority may not make a determination under this section.
(5) A class of dwellings may be prescribed under subsection (4) by reference to such factors as the Welsh Ministers think fit and may, amongst other factors, be prescribed by reference to—
   (a) the physical characteristics of, or other matters relating to, dwellings;
   (b) the circumstances of, or other matters relating to, any person who is liable to the amount of council tax concerned.
(6) Where a determination under this section has effect in relation to a class of dwellings—
   (a) the billing authority may not make a determination under section 12. (3) or (4) in relation to that class, and
   (b) any determination that has been made under section 12. (3) or (4) ceases to have effect in relation to that class.
(7) A billing authority may make a determination varying or revoking a determination under this section for a financial year, but only before the beginning of the year.
(8) Where a billing authority makes a determination under this section it must publish a notice of the determination in at least one newspaper circulating in its area.
(9) The notice must be published before the end of the period of 21 days beginning with the date of the determination.
(10) The validity of a determination is not affected by a failure to comply with subsection (8) or (9).
(11) For the purposes of this section, a dwelling is a "long-term empty dwelling" on any day if for a continuous period of at least 1 year ending with that day—
   (a) it has been unoccupied, and

(b) it has been substantially unfurnished.

(12) In determining whether a dwelling is a long-term empty dwelling, no account is to be taken of—

(a) any period which pre-dates the coming into force of this section;

(b) any one or more periods of not more than 6 weeks during which one or both of the conditions in subsection (11) are not met.

(13) The Welsh Ministers may by regulations—

(a) substitute a different percentage limit for the limit which is for the time being specified in subsection (1)(b);

(b) substitute a different period, of not less than 1 year, for the period which is for the time being specified in subsection (11);

(c) substitute a different period, of not less than 6 weeks, for the period which is for the time being specified in subsection (12)(b).

(14) A statutory instrument containing regulations made under subsection (13)(a) or (b) may not be made unless a draft of the instrument has been laid before, and approved by resolution of, the National Assembly for Wales.

(15) Any other statutory instrument containing regulations made under this section is subject to annulment in pursuance of a resolution of the National Assembly for Wales.

12. BHigher amount for dwellings occupied periodically: Wales

(1) For any financial year, a billing authority in Wales may by determination provide in relation to its area that if on any day the conditions mentioned in subsection (2) are satisfied in respect of a dwelling—

(a) the discount under section 11. (2)(a) does not apply, and

(b) the amount of council tax payable in respect of that dwelling and that day is increased by such percentage of not more than 100 as it may specify in the determination.

(2) The conditions are—

(a) there is no resident of the dwelling, and

(b) the dwelling is substantially furnished.

(3) But a billing authority's first determination under this section must be made at least one year before the beginning of the financial year to which it relates.

(4) In exercising its functions under this section a billing authority must have regard to any guidance issued by the Welsh Ministers.

(5) The Welsh Ministers may by regulations prescribe one or more classes of dwelling in relation to which a billing authority may not make a determination under this section.

(6) A class of dwellings may be prescribed under subsection (5) by reference to such factors as the Welsh Ministers think fit and may, amongst other factors, be prescribed by reference to—

(a) the physical characteristics of, or other matters relating to, dwellings;

(b) the circumstances of, or other matters relating to, any person who is liable to the amount of council tax concerned.

(7) Where a determination under this section has effect in relation to a class of dwellings—

(a) the billing authority may not make a determination under section 12. (3) or (4) in relation to that class, and

(b) any determination that has been made under section 12. (3) or (4) ceases to have effect in relation to that class.

(8) A billing authority may make a determination varying or revoking a determination under this section for a financial year, but only before the beginning of the year.

(9) Where a billing authority makes a determination under this section it must publish a notice of the determination in at least one newspaper circulating in its area.

(10) The notice must be published before the end of the period of 21 days beginning with the date of the determination.

(11) The validity of a determination is not affected by a failure to comply with subsection (9) or (10).
(12) The Welsh Ministers may by regulations specify a different percentage limit for the limit which is for the time being specified in subsection (1)(b).
(13) A statutory instrument containing regulations made under subsection (12) may not be made unless a draft of the instrument has been laid before, and approved by resolution of, the National Assembly for Wales.
(14) Any other statutory instrument containing regulations made under this section is subject to annulment in pursuance of a resolution of the National Assembly for Wales."
(3) Part 4 of Schedule 3 makes consequential amendments relating to this Part.
Commencement Information
I1. S. 139 in force at 16.12.2015 for specified purposes by S.I. 2015/2046, art. 2
I2. S. 139 in force at 1.4.2016 in so far as not already in force by S.I. 2015/2046, art. 2

PART 8. AMENDMENT OF THE LEASEHOLD REFORM, HOUSING AND URBAN DEVELOPMENT ACT 1993

PART 8 AMENDMENT OF THE LEASEHOLD REFORM, HOUSING AND URBAN DEVELOPMENT ACT 1993

140. Amendment of the Leasehold Reform, Housing and Urban Development Act 1993.

(1) In section 99. (5) of the Leasehold Reform, Housing and Urban Development Act 1993 (requirement for notices under Act to be signed by tenants or tenant personally) for paragraphs (a) and (b) substitute " be signed by or on behalf of each of the tenants, or (as the case may be) by or on behalf of the tenant, by whom it is given. "
(2) Accordingly, the Leasehold Reform (Amendment) Act 2014 is repealed.
Commencement Information
I1. S. 140 in force at 1.12.2014 by S.I. 2014/3127, art. 2. (a), Sch. Pt. 1

PART 9. MISCELLANEOUS AND GENERAL

PART 9 MISCELLANEOUS AND GENERAL

141. Minor amendments to the Mobile Homes (Wales) Act 2013.

Part 5 of Schedule 3 makes minor amendments to the Mobile Homes (Wales) Act 2013.
Commencement Information
I1. S. 141 in force at 1.12.2014 by S.I. 2014/3127, art. 2. (a), Sch. Pt. 1

General

142. Orders and regulations

(1) A power to make an order or regulations under this Act is to be exercised by statutory instrument.
(2) A power to make an order or regulations under this Act includes power—
    (a) to make different provision for different cases or classes of case, different areas or different purposes;
    (b) to make different provision generally or subject to specified exemptions or exceptions or only in relation to specific cases or classes of case;
    (c) to make such incidental, supplementary, consequential, transitory, transitional or saving provision as the person making the order or regulations considers appropriate.
(3) A statutory instrument containing any of the following may not be made unless a draft of the instrument has been laid before, and approved by resolution of, the National Assembly for Wales—
    (a) in Part 1—
(i) an order made under section 2. (1)(c), 3, 5. (f), 6. (3), 7. (4), 8. (f), 10. (4)(d), 12. (3)(d), 14. (3), 20. (7) or 29. (5);
(ii) regulations made under section 19. (2);
    (b) in Part 2—
(i) an order made under section 57. (4), 59. (3), 72, 80. (5)(b)(i), 80. (8) or 81. (4);
(ii) regulations made under section 78. (1) or 86. (1) and regulations made by the Welsh Ministers under paragraph 1 of Schedule 2;
    (c) in Part 3, an order made under section 101 or 109;
    (d) in this Part, regulations made under section 144 which amend or repeal any provision of an Act of Parliament or a Measure or Act of the National Assembly for Wales.
(4) Any other statutory instrument containing an order or regulations made by the Welsh Ministers under this Act other than an order made under section 40. (7) is subject to annulment in pursuance of a resolution of the National Assembly for Wales.
(5) A statutory instrument containing an order made under section 80. (5)(b)(ii) may not be made unless a draft of the instrument has been laid before, and approved by resolution of—
    (a) each House of Parliament, and
    (b) the National Assembly for Wales.
(6) A statutory instrument containing regulations made by the Secretary of State under paragraph 1 of Schedule 2 may not be made unless a draft of the instrument has been laid before, and approved by resolution of, each House of Parliament.
(7) This section does not apply to an order made under section 145 (commencement).

143. Meaning of local housing authority

In this Act "local housing authority" means the council of a county or county borough in Wales, and it has an extended meaning for the purposes of Part 2 (see section 99).
Prospective

144. Power to make consequential and transitional provision etc

(1) If the Welsh Ministers consider it necessary or expedient for the purpose of, or in consequence of, giving full effect to any provision of this Act, they may by regulations make—
    (a) any supplementary, incidental or consequential provision, and
    (b) any transitional or saving provision.

(2) Regulations under this section may (among other things) amend, repeal or revoke any enactment.
(3) In this section "enactment" means an enactment (whenever enacted or made) comprised in, or in an instrument made under—
(a) an Act of Parliament,
(b) a Measure or an Act of the National Assembly for Wales (including a provision of this Act).

145. Commencement

(1) The following provisions come into force on the day on which this Act receives Royal Assent—
(a) section 142;
(b) section 143;
(c) this section;
(d) section 146.
(2) Sections 132 to 136 in Part 5 (Housing Finance) come into force after the end of the period of 2 months beginning with the day on which this Act receives Royal Assent.
(3) The remaining provisions of this Act are to come into force on a day appointed by the Welsh Ministers in an order made by statutory instrument.
(4) An order under this section may—
(a) appoint different days for different purposes;
(b) include such transitory, transitional or saving provision as the Welsh Ministers consider appropriate.

146. Short title

The short title of this Act is the Housing (Wales) Act 2014.

Schedules

Schedule 1. REGISTER OF PRIVATE RENTED HOUSING

(introduced by section 14)

PART 1 CONTENT OF REGISTER

Landlords

1. An entry in the register relating to a landlord must record the following—
(a) the name of the landlord;
(b) if the landlord is a body corporate, the address of the landlord's registered or principal office;
(c) the address of each rental property in the licensing authority's area for which the landlord is the landlord;
(d) the name and licence number of any person appointed by the landlord to carry out lettings work or property management work on behalf of the landlord and the address of each rental

property to which the appointment relates;
(e) the landlord's registration number;
(f) the date the landlord was registered;
(g) where a licence has been granted to the landlord—
(i) the date the licence was granted or is renewed;
(ii) the licence number;
(iii) whether the licence has been amended under section 24; and if it has the date the amendment took effect;
(iv) whether the licence has expired without being renewed, or has been revoked; and if it has the date of expiry or revocation;
(h) where an application by the landlord for a licence has been refused by the licensing authority—
(i) the date of the refusal;
(ii) whether the refusal was appealed under section 27;
(i) where the licensing authority's refusal of an application was appealed, if the tribunal or court confirmed the authority's decision, the date of that decision;
(j) where a residential property tribunal has made a rent stopping order (see section 30) in respect of a rental property for which the landlord is the landlord—
(i) that such an order has been made;
(ii) the date the order took effect;
(iii) the date on which the order ceased to have effect (see section 31).
Commencement Information
I1. Sch. 1 para. 1 in force at 23.11.2015 by S.I. 2015/1826, art. 2. (d)

Agents

2. An entry in the register for a person licensed to carry out lettings work and property management work on behalf of a landlord must record the following—
(a) the name of the person;
(b) the correspondence address of the person;
(c) if the person is a body corporate, the address of the person's registered or principal office;
(d) if the person is carrying out lettings work and property management work on behalf of a landlord in the course of a business, the address of any premises in the area of the licensing authority used for that purpose;
(e) where a licence has been granted to the person by the licensing authority—
(i) the date the licence was granted;
(ii) the licence number;
(iii) whether the licence has been amended under section 24; and if so the date on which the amendment took effect;
(f) where an application by the person for a licence has been refused by the licensing authority—
(i) the date of the refusal;
(ii) whether the refusal was appealed under section 27;
(g) where the licensing authority's refusal of an application was appealed, if the tribunal or court confirmed the authority's decision, the date of that decision.
Commencement Information
I2. Sch. 1 para. 2 in force at 23.11.2015 by S.I. 2015/1826, art. 2. (d)

PART 2 ACCESS TO REGISTER

3. (1) A licensing authority must notify a person of the information mentioned in sub-paragraph (2) if that person makes a request for the information and provides the authority with the address of a rental property which is on its register.
(2) The information is—

(a) the name of the landlord of the property and the name of any person appointed to carry out lettings work and property management work on behalf of the landlord in relation to the property;
(b) whether the landlord or person appointed to carry out lettings work and property management work on behalf of the landlord (as applicable) is licensed;
(c) if a rent stopping order under section 30 is in effect in relation to the property, that such an order is in effect.

Commencement Information

I3. Sch. 1 para. 3 in force at 23.11.2015 by S.I. 2015/1826, art. 2. (d)

4. (1)A licensing authority must notify a person of the information mentioned in sub-paragraph (2) if that person makes a request for the information and provides the authority with—
(a) the name of a landlord of a rental property in an area for which the authority is the licensing authority, or
(b) the name of a person appointed to carry out lettings work and property management work on behalf of the landlord in relation to any such property.
(2) The information is—
(a) whether the landlord is registered;
(b) whether the landlord or person appointed to carry out lettings work and property management work on behalf of the landlord (as applicable) is licensed.

Commencement Information

I4. Sch. 1 para. 4 in force at 23.11.2015 by S.I. 2015/1826, art. 2. (d)

5. (1)A licensing authority must notify a person of the information mentioned in sub-paragraph (2) if that person requests the information and provides the authority with—
(a) the registration number or licence number of a landlord of a rental property in the area for which the authority is the licensing authority, or
(b) the licence number of a person appointed to carry out lettings work and property management work on behalf of a landlord in relation to any such property.
(2) The information is—
(a) the name of the landlord and any person appointed to carry out lettings work and property management work on behalf of the landlord (as applicable);
(b) whether the landlord is registered;
(c) whether the landlord or any person appointed to carry out lettings work and property management work on behalf of the landlord (as applicable) is licensed.

Commencement Information

I5. Sch. 1 para. 5 in force at 23.11.2015 by S.I. 2015/1826, art. 2. (d)

Schedule 2. ELIGIBILITY FOR HELP UNDER CHAPTER 2 OF PART 2

(introduced by section 61)

Persons not eligible for help

1. (1)A person is not eligible for help under section 66, 68, 73 or 75 if he or she is a person from abroad who is ineligible for housing assistance.
(2) A person who is subject to immigration control within the meaning of the Asylum and Immigration Act 1996 is not eligible for housing assistance unless the person falls within a class of persons prescribed by regulations made by the Welsh Ministers or the Secretary of State.
(3) No person who is excluded from entitlement to universal credit or housing benefit by section 115 of the Immigration and Asylum Act 1999 (exclusion from benefits) may be included in any class prescribed under sub-paragraph (2).

(4) The Welsh Ministers or the Secretary of State may by regulations provide for other descriptions of persons who are to be treated for the purposes of Chapter 2 of Part 2 as persons from abroad who are ineligible for housing assistance.

(5) A person who is not eligible for housing assistance is to be disregarded in determining for the purposes of Chapter 2 of Part 2 whether a person falling within sub-paragraph (6)—

(a) is homeless or threatened with homelessness, or

(b) has a priority need for accommodation.

(6) A person falls within this subsection if the person—

(a) falls within a class prescribed by regulations made under sub-paragraph (2), and

(b) is not a national of an EEA State or Switzerland.

Commencement Information

I1. Sch. 2 para. 1 in force at 1.12.2014 for specified purposes by S.I. 2014/3127, art. 2. (b), Sch. Pt. 2

I2. Sch. 2 para. 1 in force at 27.4.2015 in so far as not already in force by S.I. 2015/1272, art. 2, Sch. para. 52 (with art. 5)

Asylum-seekers and their dependants: transitional provision

2. (1)Until the commencement of the repeal of section 186 of the Housing Act 1996 (asylum-seekers and their dependants), that section applies to Chapter 2 of Part 2 of this Act as it applies to Part 7 of that Act.

(2) For this purpose, in section 186 of the Housing Act 1996—

(a) the reference to section 185 of that Act is to be interpreted as a reference to paragraph 1, and

(b) the reference to "this Part" is to be interpreted as a reference to Chapter 2 of Part 2 of this Act and not Part 7 of that Act.

Commencement Information

I3. Sch. 2 para. 2 in force at 27.4.2015 by S.I. 2015/1272, art. 2, Sch. para. 52 (with art. 5)

Provision of information by Secretary of State

3. (1)The Secretary of State must, at the request of a local housing authority, provide the authority with such information as it may require—

(a) as to whether a person is a person to whom section 115 of the Immigration and Asylum Act 1999 (exclusion from benefits) applies, and

(b) to enable it to determine whether such a person is eligible for help under Chapter 2 of Part 2.

(2) Where that information is given otherwise than in writing, the Secretary of State must confirm it in writing if a written request is made to the Secretary of State by the authority.

(3) If it appears to the Secretary of State that any application, decision or other change of circumstances has affected the status of a person about whom information was previously provided to a local housing authority under this paragraph, the Secretary of State must inform the authority in writing of that fact, the reason for it and the date on which the previous information became inaccurate.

Commencement Information

I4. Sch. 2 para. 3 in force at 27.4.2015 by S.I. 2015/1272, art. 2, Sch. para. 52 (with art. 5)

Schedule 3. MINOR AND CONSEQUENTIAL AMENDMENTS

(as introduced by sections, 100, 110, 130, 139 and 141)

PART 1 HOMELESSNESS

Housing Act 1985.

1. In paragraph 4 of Schedule 1 to the Housing Act 1985 (tenancies which are not secure tenancies), after "(homelessness)" insert " or Part 2 of the Housing (Wales) Act 2014 (homelessness) ".
Commencement Information
I1. Sch. 3 para. 1 in force at 27.4.2015 by S.I. 2015/1272, art. 2, Sch. para. 53 (with art. 7)

Housing Act 1996.

2. The Housing Act 1996 is amended as follows.
Commencement Information
I2. Sch. 3 para. 2 in force at 27.4.2015 by S.I. 2015/1272, art. 2, Sch. para. 53 (with art. 7)
3. In section 167 (allocation of housing accommodation in accordance with allocation scheme: Wales)—
(a) in subsection (2)—
(i) in paragraph (a), for "(within the meaning of Part 7)" substitute " (within the meaning of Part 2 of the Housing (Wales) Act 2014) ";
(ii) for paragraph (b) substitute—
"(b)people who are owed any duty by a local housing authority under section 66, 73 or 75 of the Housing (Wales) Act 2014;"
(b) in subsection (2. ZA), for "Part 7" substitute " Part 2 of the Housing (Wales) Act 2014 ";
(c) in subsection (2. A)(c), for "section 199" substitute " section 81 of the Housing (Wales) Act 2014 ".
Commencement Information
I3. Sch. 3 para. 3 in force at 27.4.2015 by S.I. 2015/1272, art. 2, Sch. para. 53 (with art. 7)
4. In the Part title of Part 7 (homelessness), after "Homelessness" insert " : England ".
Commencement Information
I4. Sch. 3 para. 4 in force at 27.4.2015 by S.I. 2015/1272, art. 2, Sch. para. 53 (with art. 7)
5. In subsection (1) of section 179 (duty of local housing authority to provide advisory services), after "local housing authority" insert " in England ".
Commencement Information
I5. Sch. 3 para. 5 in force at 27.4.2015 by S.I. 2015/1272, art. 2, Sch. para. 53 (with art. 7)
6. In subsection (1) of section 180 (assistance for voluntary organisations), after "local housing authority" insert " in England ".
Commencement Information
I6. Sch. 3 para. 6 in force at 27.4.2015 by S.I. 2015/1272, art. 2, Sch. para. 53 (with art. 7)
7. In subsection (1) of section 182 (guidance by the Secretary of State), after "social services authority" insert " in England ".
Commencement Information
I7. Sch. 3 para. 7 in force at 27.4.2015 by S.I. 2015/1272, art. 2, Sch. para. 53 (with art. 7)
8. In subsection (1) of section 183 (application for assistance), after "local housing authority" insert " in England ".
Commencement Information
I8. Sch. 3 para. 8 in force at 27.4.2015 by S.I. 2015/1272, art. 2, Sch. para. 53 (with art. 7)
9. In subsection (1) of section 187 (provision of information by Secretary of State), after "local housing authority" insert " in England ".

Commencement Information
I9. Sch. 3 para. 9 in force at 27.4.2015 by S.I. 2015/1272, art. 2, Sch. para. 53 (with art. 7)
10. In section 193 (duty to persons with priority need who are not homeless intentionally)—
(a) in subsection (10), for "appropriate authority" substitute " Secretary of State ";
(b) omit subsection (12).
Commencement Information
I10. Sch. 3 para. 10 in force at 27.4.2015 by S.I. 2015/1272, art. 2, Sch. para. 53 (with art. 7)
11. In section 198 (referral of case to another local housing authority)—
(a) after subsection (4) insert—
"(4. A)Subsection (4) is to be construed, in a case where the other authority is an authority in Wales, as if the reference to "this Part" were a reference to Part 2 of the Housing (Wales) Act 2014."
(b) in subsection (5), after "case" insert " which does not involve a referral to a local housing authority in Wales ";
(c) after that subsection, insert—
"(5. A)The question whether the conditions for referral of a case involving a referral to a local housing authority in Wales shall be decided by agreement between the notifying authority and the notified authority or, in default of agreement, in accordance with such arrangements as the Secretary of State and the Welsh Ministers may jointly direct by order.";
(d) in subsection (6)(b), after "Secretary of State" insert " or, in the case of an order under subsection (5. A), to the Secretary of State and the Welsh Ministers ";
(e) in subsection (7)—
(i) for "No such order shall" substitute " An order under this section shall not "; and
(ii) at the end, insert " and, in the case of a joint order, a resolution of the National Assembly for Wales ".
Commencement Information
I11. Sch. 3 para. 11 in force at 27.4.2015 by S.I. 2015/1272, art. 2, Sch. para. 53 (with art. 7)
12. In subsection (4) of section 200 (duties to applicant whose case is considered for referral or referred)—
(a) after "met" insert " and the notified authority is not an authority in Wales ", and
(b) at the end, insert " ; for provision about cases where it is decided that those conditions are met and the notified authority is an authority in Wales, see section 83 of the Housing (Wales) Act 2014 (cases referred from a local housing authority in England) ".
Commencement Information
I12. Sch. 3 para. 12 in force at 27.4.2015 by S.I. 2015/1272, art. 2, Sch. para. 53 (with art. 7)
13. After section 201 (application of referral provisions to cases arising in Scotland) insert—
"201. ACases referred from a local housing authority in Wales
(1) This section applies where an application has been referred by a local housing authority in Wales to a local housing authority in England under section 80 of the Housing (Wales) Act 2014 (referral of case to another local housing authority).
(2) If it is decided that the conditions in that section for referral of the case are met, the notified authority are subject to the duty under section 193 of this Act in respect of the person whose case is referred (the main housing duty); for provision about cases where it is decided that the conditions for referral are not met, see section 82 of the Housing (Wales) Act 2014 (duties to applicant whose case is considered for referral or referred).
(3) References in this Part to an applicant include a reference to a person to whom a duty is owed by virtue of subsection (2)."
Commencement Information
I13. Sch. 3 para. 13 in force at 27.4.2015 by S.I. 2015/1272, art. 2, Sch. para. 53 (with art. 7)
14. In subsection (1) of section 213 (co-operation between relevant housing authorities and bodies), after "local housing authority" insert " in England ".
Commencement Information
I14. Sch. 3 para. 14 in force at 27.4.2015 by S.I. 2015/1272, art. 2, Sch. para. 53 (with art. 7)

Homelessness Act 2002.

15. The Homelessness Act 2002 is amended as follows.
Commencement Information
I15. Sch. 3 para. 15 in force at 27.4.2015 by S.I. 2015/1272, art. 2, Sch. para. 53 (with art. 7)
16. In the cross-heading above section 1, after "strategies" insert " : England ".
Commencement Information
I16. Sch. 3 para. 16 in force at 27.4.2015 by S.I. 2015/1272, art. 2, Sch. para. 53 (with art. 7)
17. In section 1 (duty of local housing authority to formulate a homelessness strategy)—
(a) in subsections (1) and (5), after "local housing authority" insert " in England ";
(b) in the heading, after "local housing authority" insert " in England ".
Commencement Information
I17. Sch. 3 para. 17 in force at 27.4.2015 by S.I. 2015/1272, art. 2, Sch. para. 53 (with art. 7)
18. In subsection (7. A) of section 3 (homelessness strategies), omit "in England".
Commencement Information
I18. Sch. 3 para. 18 in force at 27.4.2015 by S.I. 2015/1272, art. 2, Sch. para. 53 (with art. 7)

Mental Health (Wales) Measure 2010.

19. In subsection (1)(a) of section 50 of the Mental Health (Wales) Measure 2010 (meaning of housing or well-being services), for "Part 7 of that Act" substitute " Part 2 of the Housing (Wales) Act 2014 ".
Commencement Information
I19. Sch. 3 para. 19 in force at 27.4.2015 by S.I. 2015/1272, art. 2, Sch. para. 53 (with art. 7)

Legal Aid, Sentencing and Punishment of Offenders Act 2012.

20. (1)The Legal Aid, Sentencing and Punishment of Offenders Act 2012 is amended as follows.
(2) In paragraph 34 of Part 1 of Schedule 1 (homelessness)—
(a) in sub-paragraph (1), after paragraph (b) insert—
   "(c)Part 2 of the Housing (Wales) Act 2014 (homelessness).";
(b) in sub-paragraph (3) for "as in section 175 of the Housing Act 1996" substitute "—
   (a) as in section 175 of the Housing Act 1996 in cases where sub-paragraph (1) applies in relation to the provision of accommodation and assistance under—
(i) Part 6 of that Act as it relates to England;
(ii) Part 7 of that Act;
   (b) as in section 55 of the Housing (Wales) Act 2014 in cases where sub-paragraph (1) applies in relation to the provision of accommodation and assistance under—
(i) Part 6 of the Housing Act 1996 as it relates to Wales;
(ii) Part 2 of the Housing (Wales) Act 2014."
Commencement Information
I20. Sch. 3 para. 20 in force at 27.4.2015 by S.I. 2015/1272, art. 2, Sch. para. 53 (with art. 7)

Prevention of Social Housing Fraud Act 2013.

21. In subsection (7)(d) of section 7 of the Prevention of Social Housing Fraud Act 2013 (regulations about powers to require information), after "Housing Act 1996" insert " or under Part 2 of the Housing (Wales) Act 2014 ".
Commencement Information
I21. Sch. 3 para. 21 in force at 27.4.2015 by S.I. 2015/1272, art. 2, Sch. para. 53 (with art. 7)

Social Services and Well-being (Wales) Act 2014.

22. (1)The Social Services and Well-being (Wales) Act 2014 is amended as follows.
(2) In paragraph (a) of section 48 (exception for provision of housing etc), for "Housing Act 1996" substitute " Housing (Wales) Act 2014 ".
(3) In the table in Schedule 2 (social services functions)—
(a) omit the entry for the Housing Act 1996;
(b) after the entry for the Care Act 2014 insert—
"Housing (Wales) Act 2014 Section 95. (2), (3) and (4); but only where those functions apply by virtue of subsection (5)(b) of that section.
Commencement Information
I22. Sch. 3 para. 22 in force at 27.4.2015 by S.I. 2015/1272, art. 2, Sch. para. 53 (with art. 7)

PART 2 GYPSIES AND TRAVELLERS

Local Government Act 2003.

23. (1)The definition of "housing" in subsection (4) of section 87 of the Local Government Act 2003 (housing strategies and statements) is amended as follows—
(a) omit the words "section 225 of the Housing Act 2004", and
(b) after "of" where it first occurs insert—
"(a)section 225 of the Housing Act 2004, in the case of a local housing authority in England;
(b) Part 3 of the Housing (Wales) Act 2014, in the case of a local housing authority in Wales."
Commencement Information
I23. Sch. 3 para. 23 in force at 25.2.2015 by S.I. 2015/380, art. 2. (h)

Housing Act 2004.

24. (1)The Housing Act 2004 is amended as follows.
(2) In section 225 (duties of local housing authorities: accommodation needs of Gypsies and Travellers)—
(a) in subsection (1), after "local housing authority" insert " in England ",
(b) in subsection (2), after "local housing authority" insert " in England ",
(c) in the definition of "gypsies and travellers" in subsection (5), for "appropriate national authority" substitute " Secretary of State ", and
(d) in the heading, after "local housing authorities" insert " in England ".
(3) In subsection (1) of section 226 (guidance in relation to section 225)—
(a) for "appropriate national authority" substitute " Secretary of State ", and
(b) after "local housing authorities" where it first occurs insert " in England ".
Commencement Information
I24. Sch. 3 para. 24 in force at 25.2.2015 by S.I. 2015/380, art. 2. (h)

Housing (Assessment of Accommodation Needs) (Meaning of Gypsies and Travellers) (Wales) Regulations 2007 (S.I. 2007/3235)

25. The Housing (Assessment of Accommodation Needs) (Meaning of Gypsies and Travellers) (Wales) Regulations 2007 (S.I. 2007/3235) are revoked.
Commencement Information

I25. Sch. 3 para. 25 in force at 25.2.2015 by S.I. 2015/380, art. 2. (h)

Mobile Homes (Wales) Act 2013.

26. (1)The Mobile Homes (Wales) Act 2013 is amended as follows.
(2) In the definition of "Gypsies and Travellers" in section 62 (other interpretation), for the words from "persons" where it first occurs to the end substitute "—
(a) persons of a nomadic habit of life, whatever their race or origin, including—
    (i) persons who, on grounds only of their own or their family's or dependant's educational needs or old age, have ceased to travel temporarily or permanently, and
    (ii) members of an organised group of travelling show people or circus people (whether or not travelling together as such); and
(b) all other persons with a cultural tradition of nomadism or of living in a mobile home;".
(3) In sub-paragraph (1) of paragraph 10 of Schedule 1 (travelling showmen), after "a" where it first occurs insert " non-local authority owned ".
Commencement Information
I26. Sch. 3 para. 26 in force at 25.2.2015 by S.I. 2015/380, art. 2. (h)

PART 3 STANDARDS FOR SOCIAL HOUSING

Housing Act 1985.

27. In section 24 (rents for occupation of local housing authority houses) of the Housing Act 1985—
(a) omit subsections (3) and (4);
(b) after subsection (5), insert—
"(6)In exercising its functions under this section, a local housing authority in Wales must—
    (a) comply with any standards relating to rent or service charges which are set for it under section 111 of the Housing (Wales) Act 2014, and
    (b) have regard to any guidance relating to rent or service charges which is issued under section 112 of that Act."
Commencement Information
I27. Sch. 3 para. 27 in force at 1.12.2014 by S.I. 2014/3127, art. 2. (a), Sch. Pt. 1

Housing Act 1996.

28. (1)The Housing Act 1996 is amended as follows.
(2) In section 33. A (standards of performance to be met by registered social landlords) after subsection (2), insert—
"(2. A)Standards set under subsection (1) may require registered social landlords to comply with rules specified in the standards.
(2. B)The Welsh Ministers may—
    (a) revise the standards by issuing further standards under this section;
    (b) withdraw the standards by issuing further standards under this section or by notice.
(2. C)The Welsh Ministers must publish any standards or notice under this section."
(3) In section 33. B (guidance from Welsh Ministers on standards for registered social landlords)—
(a) for subsection (3) substitute—
"(3)The Welsh Ministers may—
    (a) revise the guidance by issuing further guidance under this section;

(b) withdraw the guidance by issuing further guidance under this section or by notice."
(b) for subsection (4) substitute—
"(4)The Welsh Ministers must publish any guidance or notice under this section."
(4) In section 33. C (consultation before setting standards for registered social landlords or issuing guidance on standards), after "setting" insert " , revising or withdrawing ".
Commencement Information
I28. Sch. 3 para. 28 in force at 1.12.2014 by S.I. 2014/3127, art. 2. (a), Sch. Pt. 1

PART 4 COUNCIL TAX FOR CERTAIN TYPES OF DWELLING

Local Government Finance Act 1992.

29. (1)The Local Government Finance Act 1992 is amended as follows.
(2) In section 11. (2) (discounts), for "and 12" substitute " , 12, 12. A and 12. B ".
(3) In section 12 (discounts: special provision for Wales), after subsection (4) insert—
"(4. A)Subsections (3) and (4) are subject to section 12. A(6) and 12. B(7)."
(4) In section 13. (3) (reduced amounts), for "or 12" substitute " , 12, 12. A or 12. B ".
(5) In section 66. (2)(b) (judicial review), for "or 12" substitute " , 12, 12. A or 12. B ".
(6) In section 67. (2)(a) (functions to be discharged only by authority), for "or 12" substitute " , 12, 12. A or 12. B ".
(7) In Schedule 2 (administration), in paragraph 4. (7) for "(higher amount of tax for empty dwellings)" substitute " (higher amount of tax for empty dwellings: England), 12. A(1)(b) (higher amount of tax for empty dwellings: Wales) or 12. B(1)(b) (higher amount of tax for dwellings occupied periodically: Wales) ".
Commencement Information
I29. Sch. 3 para. 29 in force at 16.12.2015 for specified purposes by S.I. 2015/2046, art. 2
I30. Sch. 3 para. 29 in force at 1.4.2016 in so far as not already in force by S.I. 2015/2046, art. 2

PART 5 AMENDMENTS TO THE MOBILE HOMES (WALES) ACT 2013

30. (1)The Mobile Homes (Wales) Act 2013 is amended as follows.
(2) In section 29. (3) (decision whether a person is fit and proper to manage a site), for paragraph (b) substitute—
"(b)practised unlawful discrimination or harassment on the grounds of any characteristic which is a protected characteristic under section 4 of the Equality Act 2010, or victimised another person contrary to that Act, in or in connection with the carrying on of any business, or".
(3) In section 33 (repayment orders)—
(a) omit subsection (7);
(b) in subsection (8) for "(11)" substitute " (10) ";
(c) in subsection (9)(c) for "at any time" substitute " previously ".
(4) In section 39. (1) (interpretation of Part 2) omit the definition of "fire and rescue authority" and insert it into section 62 (other interpretation) at the appropriate place.
(5) In section 49. (4) (particulars of mobile home agreements) for "Act" substitute " Part ".
(6) In section 53. (4) (successors in title) for "Act" substitute " Part ".
(7) In section 61. (7) (meaning of "qualifying residents' association") omit the definitions of "arbitration agreement" and "tribunal".
Commencement Information
I31. Sch. 3 para. 30 in force at 1.12.2014 by S.I. 2014/3127, art. 2. (a), Sch. Pt. 1

Open Government Licence v3.0

Contains public sector information licensed under the Open Government Licence v3.0. The full licence if available at the following address:
http://www.nationalarchives.gov.uk/doc/open-government-licence/version/3/

Printed in Great Britain
by Amazon